Lives That Resist Telling

Lives That Resist Telling challenges the resounding scholarly silence about the lives of migrant women who identify as lesbian, queer, or nonheteronormative. Reworking social science methodologies and theories, the essays explore the experiences of migrant Latina lesbians in Los Angeles; Latina lesbians whose transnational lives span the borders between the United States and Mexico; non-heteronormative migrant Muslim women in Norway and Denmark; economically privileged Chinese lesbian or *lala* women in Australia; and Iranian lesbian asylum-seekers in Turkey. The authors show how state migration controls and multiple institutions of power try to subjectify and govern migrant lesbians in often contradictory ways, and how migrant lesbians cope, strategize, and respond.

The essays complicate and rework binaries of visibility/invisibility, in/out, victim/agent, home/homeless, and belonging/unbelonging. Tellability emerges as a technology of power and violence, and conversely, as a mode of healing, (re)building a sense of self and connection to others, and creating conditions for livability and queer world-making.

This book was first published as a special issue of the *Journal of Lesbian Studies*.

Eithne Luibhéid is Professor of Gender and Women's Studies at the University of Arizona, Tucson, USA. She is the author of *Pregnant on Arrival: Making the 'Illegal' Immigrant* (University of Minnesota Press, 2013) and *Entry Denied: Controlling Sexuality at the Border* (University of Minnesota Press, 2002); and the co-editor of *Queer and Trans Migrations: Dynamics of Illegalization, Detention, and Deportation* (University of Illinois Press, 2020).

Lives That Resist Telling
Migrant and Refugee Lesbians

Edited by
Eithne Luibhéid

LONDON AND NEW YORK

First published 2021
by Routledge
2 Park Square, Milton Park, Abingdon, Oxon, OX14 4RN

and by Routledge
52 Vanderbilt Avenue, New York, NY 10017

Routledge is an imprint of the Taylor & Francis Group, an informa business

Chapters 1–3, 5 and 6 © 2021 Taylor & Francis
Chapter 4 © 2019 Mia Liinason. Originally published as Open Access.

With the exception of Chapter 4, no part of this book may be reprinted or reproduced or utilised in any form or by any electronic, mechanical, or other means, now known or hereafter invented, including photocopying and recording, or in any information storage or retrieval system, without permission in writing from the publishers. For details on the rights for Chapter 4, please see the chapter's Open Access footnote.

Trademark notice: Product or corporate names may be trademarks or registered trademarks, and are used only for identification and explanation without intent to infringe.

British Library Cataloguing-in-Publication Data
A catalogue record for this book is available from the British Library

ISBN13: 978-0-367-69536-1 (hbk)
ISBN13: 978-1-003-14217-1 (ebk)

Typeset in Minion Pro
by codeMantra

Publisher's Note
The publisher accepts responsibility for any inconsistencies that may have arisen during the conversion of this book from journal articles to book chapters, namely the inclusion of journal terminology.

Disclaimer
Every effort has been made to contact copyright holders for their permission to reprint material in this book. The publishers would be grateful to hear from any copyright holder who is not here acknowledged and will undertake to rectify any errors or omissions in future editions of this book.

Contents

Citation Information vi
Notes on Contributors viii

1. Migrant and refugee lesbians: Lives that resist the telling 1
   Eithne Luibhéid

2. Finding sequins in the rubble: The journeys of two Latina migrant lesbians in Los Angeles 21
   Eddy Francisco Alvarez, Jr.

3. "We have to do *a lot* of healing": LGBTQ migrant Latinas resisting and healing from systemic violence 38
   Sandibel Borges

4. Challenging the visibility paradigm: Tracing ambivalences in lesbian migrant women's negotiations of sexual identity 54
   Mia Liinason

5. Coming out and going abroad: The *chuguo* mobility of queer women in China 70
   Lucetta Y. L. Kam

6. Lesbian refugees in transit: The making of authenticity and legitimacy in Turkey 84
   Elif Sarı

Index 103

Citation Information

The chapters in this book were originally published in the *Journal of Lesbian Studies*, volume 24, issue 2 (2020). When citing this material, please use the original page numbering for each article, as follows:

Chapter 1
Migrant and refugee lesbians: Lives that resist the telling
Eithne Luibhéid
Journal of Lesbian Studies, volume 24, issue 2 (2020) pp. 57–76

Chapter 2
Finding sequins in the rubble: The journeys of two Latina migrant lesbians in Los Angeles
Eddy Francisco Alvarez, Jr.
Journal of Lesbian Studies, volume 24, issue 2 (2020) pp. 77–93

Chapter 3
"We have to do a lot of healing": LGBTQ migrant Latinas resisting and healing from systemic violence
Sandibel Borges
Journal of Lesbian Studies, volume 24, issue 2 (2020) pp. 94–109

Chapter 4
Challenging the visibility paradigm: Tracing ambivalences in lesbian migrant women's negotiations of sexual identity
Mia Liinason
Journal of Lesbian Studies, volume 24, issue 2 (2020) pp. 110–125

Chapter 5
Coming out and going abroad: The chuguo *mobility of queer women in China*
Lucetta Y. L. Kam
Journal of Lesbian Studies, volume 24, issue 2 (2020) pp. 126–139

Chapter 6
Lesbian refugees in transit: The making of authenticity and legitimacy in Turkey
Elif Sarı
Journal of Lesbian Studies, volume 24, issue 2 (2020) pp. 140–158

For any permission-related enquiries please visit:
http://www.tandfonline.com/page/help/permissions

Contributors

Eddy Francisco Alvarez, Jr. is an interdisciplinary scholar focusing on Latinx queer geographies and archives, Latinx aesthetics, and Jotería studies. He is an Assistant Professor in the Department of Chicana and Chicano Studies at California State University, Fullerton. A first-generation college student and first in his family to obtain a doctorate, he holds a Ph.D. in Chicana and Chicano Studies from the University of California, Santa Barbara. His scholarly and creative work has been published in *TSQ*, *Aztlán*, *Label Me Latina/o*, and *Bilingual Review/La Revista Bilingüe*. Currently, he is working on a book manuscript titled *Finding Sequins in the Rubble: Space, Aesthetics and Memory in Queer Latinx Los Angeles* and on a project on queer, trans, and feminist fans of Mexican pop icon Gloria Trevi. He is a board member of the Association for Jotería Arts, Activism and Scholarship (AJAAS).

Sandibel Borges is Assistant Professor in Women's and Gender Studies at Loyola Marymount. She received her Ph.D. in Feminist Studies from the University of California, Santa Barbara, and was faculty in the Women's, Gender, and Sexuality Studies Program at the University of Wisconsin-Eau Claire, and a postdoctoral fellow in the Center for Mexican American Studies at the University of Texas at Austin. Her work investigates how heteronormativity, white supremacy, and exploitation are naturalized and institutionalized within migration processes, and their impact on Latinx LGBTQ migrants in Los Angeles, California and Mexico City, Mexico. Dr. Borges's work has appeared in *Women's Studies Quarterly*, the *Journal of Lesbian Studies*, *Chicana/Latina Studies: The Journal of Mujeres Activas en Letras y Cambio Social*, and *Diálogo*.

Lucetta Y. L. Kam is Associate Professor in the Department of Humanities and Creative Writing at Hong Kong Baptist University. Her research interests include queer mobility of Chinese women, *tongzhi* communities and activism in China, Hong Kong studies, and East Asian queer popular culture. She is the author of *Shanghai Lalas: Female Tongzhi Communities and Politics in Urban China* (2013; Chinese edition 2015). Her current projects include the transnational mobility of queer women from China and the lesbian fandom in Taiwan of the all-female Takarazuka Revue in Japan.

Mia Liinason is Professor in Gender Studies at the University of Gothenburg and director of TechnAct: Transformations of Struggle, a research cluster devoted to exploring the interconnections between the digital, the social, and the cultural in civil society engagements and social movements. She is interested in analyzing the relationship between resistance and power in feminism and queer scholarship and activism. Recent publications include *Equality Struggles: Feminist Movements, Neoliberal Markets and State Political Agendas* *in Scandinavia* (Routledge 2018) and, with Erika Alm, "Ungendering Europe: Critical Engagements with Key Objects in Feminism," a guest-edited section of *Gender, Place and Culture: A Journal of Feminist Geography* (25: 7, 2018). Currently, Mia is project leader of the research project Spaces of Resistance, aiming to expand our understandings of the potentials of transnational encounters in feminist and lgbti activism in Scandinavia, Russia, and Turkey.

Eithne Luibhéid is Professor of Gender and Women's Studies at the University of Arizona (UA). She holds a Ph.D. in Ethnic Studies from the University of California, Berkeley, and her research focuses on the connections among queer lives, state immigration controls, and justice struggles. She served as the Director of the Institute for LGBT Studies at UA from 2007–2011. Luibhéid is the author of *Pregnant on Arrival: Making the "Illegal" Immigrant* (University of Minnesota Press, 2013) and *Entry Denied: Controlling Sexuality at the Border* (University of Minnesota Press, 2002). She is the editor of "Queer Migrations," a special issue of *GLQ* (2008), and the co-editor of *Queer and Trans Migrations: Dynamics of "Illegalization," Detention and Deportation* (University of Illinois Press, 2020); *A Global History of Sexuality* (Wiley Blackwell, 2014); *Queer Migrations: Sexuality, Citizenship, and Border Crossings* (University of Minnesota Press, 2005); and "Representing Migrant Women in Ireland and the E.U.," a special issue of *Women's Studies International Forum* (2004). Luibhéid's current book manuscript explores how deportability is being extended and resisted through queer intimate ties.

Elif Sarı is a Ph.D. candidate in the Department of Anthropology at Cornell University. Her research interests include gender, sexuality, asylum, and humanitarianism in the Middle East. She is the co-editor of the Turkey Page at *Jadaliyya* e-zine

Migrant and refugee lesbians: Lives that resist the telling

Eithne Luibhéid

ABSTRACT
This essay introduces the special issue on "Migrant and Refugee Lesbians: Lives that Resist the Telling." It discusses the stakes involved in silence about migrant lesbian lives that permeates scholarship; reviews published works that address migrant lesbians; and highlights theoretical traditions that promise to enable further scholarship. The essay then critically explores multiple meanings associated with the terms "lesbian" and "migrant," and reviews common colonialist binaries and linear narratives that condition im/possibilities for "telling" about lesbian migrant lives. It concludes by describing the essays in the special issue, including their contributions to enabling forms of telling by highlighting multiple relations of power, and possibilities for intervention and transformation.

This special issue, centered on "Lives that Resist Telling: Migrant and Refugee Lesbians," was prompted by consistent silence in scholarship about the lives of migrant women who identify as lesbian, queer, or nonheteronormative (hereafter "lesbian"). This silence extends to queer migration scholarship, a relatively recent area of research that explores the ways that sexuality structures and is restructured by migration processes. As this special issue goes to press, no major book-length work focuses primarily on lesbian-identified migrants and many leave them out entirely. The problematic of "lives that resist telling," which draws inspiration and analytical insights from scholar Kimberlé Crenshaw (1992), asks why the lives of lesbian-identified migrants seem to remain untellable across scholarship.

Crenshaw used the phrase "lives that resist the telling" in her 1992 essay that analyzed how Black women, including law professor Anita Hill, who accused nominee and eventual Supreme Court appointee Clarence Thomas of sexual harassment, live in a "political vacuum of erasure and contradiction" (403). Crenshaw describes "existing within the overlapping margins of race and gender discourse and in the empty spaces between, [the lives of Black women are] a location whose very nature resists the telling" (403). Crenshaw is describing intersectionality, meant not in the neoliberal sense of "adding" together considerations of race, gender, class, sexuality, and citizenship status to derive understanding of someone's identity conceived as personal property, but in the sense of being located at the intersections of several nondominant positionalities, which results in "the lack of available and widely comprehended narratives to communicate the reality of [one's] experience to the world" (404). In the Hill/Thomas case, competing narratives that centered either sexism or racism, but never both, ensured that "the simultaneity of Hill's race and gender" positionality went unrepresented even as the events surrounding her were "appropriated to tell everybody's story but her own" (406) and the injustices she experienced went unaddressed. Crenshaw concludes with a call to center Black women's stories in order to come to grips with and transform how power is allocated and withheld, because "the empowerment of Black women constitutes the empowerment of our entire community" (436).

Crenshaw's analysis provided the lens through which I formulated my question about the intractable silence across scholarly fields concerning migrant lesbian experience. Following Crenshaw and others, this special issue is a call not simply to "add" consideration of lesbian experiences to migration research and activism, but also to inquire into and work toward the transformation of relations of power and knowledge that continually situate lesbian-identified migrants within erasure, silence, and violence. Lesbian migrants are heterogeneous and scholarship must therefore name and address the varying forms of erasure, silence, and violence they experience, depending the interlocking positionalities that they inhabit within contexts of neoliberalism, imperial power, and decolonial struggles. Transforming these relations opens up new spaces for considering lesbian-identified migrants' experiences and strengthens scholars' capacity to analyze how sexuality structures *all* migrant experiences in ways that normalize some while rendering others available for violence and silencing. This approach may contribute toward imagining and creating worlds where, as Loyd, Mitchelson, and Burridge (2013) describe, possibilities for some do not depend on the subordination of others.[1]

Ground on which to build

A handful of pathbreaking works that center migrant lesbians provide an inspiring foundation on which to build.[2] M. Jacqui Alexander's (1994) "Not Just Any Body Can Be a Citizen" begins: "I am an outlaw in my country of birth." She describes being raised in the Bahamas with the promise that the master's day was done, yet subsequent governments steadily betrayed that promise and revised the terms of citizenship to exclude women, including lesbians who asserted erotic autonomy. Alexander risked criminalization in the Bahamas for engaging in same-sex sexuality; as a permanent resident but not citizen in the United States, she remained at risk of criminalization for same-sex sex acts and being a Black woman migrant (5). In this essay and subsequent work (2005), Alexander incisively analyzes connections among colonial and postcolonial state-making, mandatory heterosexualization, capitalist development and migration, and contributes to their transformation

Several book-length works on queer diaspora theorize the interplay between lesbian sexualities, female genders, and international migration—especially Gloria Wekker's (2006) *The Politics of Passion*, Gayatri Gopinath's (2005) *Impossible Desires*, and Omise'eke Natasha Tinsley's (2010) *Thiefing Sugar*.[3] These luminous books rewrite accepted histories and paradigms, create methodologies for silenced lives to be considered, and open up possibilities for different futures. Although not the central focus, migrant lesbians are discussed in several book-length studies of queer migration and queer asylum (e.g., Amit 2018; Chávez 2013; El-Tayeb 2011; Giametta 2017; Kuntsman 2009; Rand 2005). They make fleeting appearances in books about supposedly heterosexual marriage migration, migrant sex work, and migrant domestic work. A handful of groundbreaking Ph.D. dissertations center lesbian migrant women, and other dissertations include them within general rubrics such as "queer" or explorations of same-sex couple migration. Growing numbers of individual articles and book chapters also explore experiences of lesbian migrant women. Some of that work centers lesbians in relation to labor migration, a largely overlooked issue until recently (Lai 2018; Muñoz 2016). Information about the lives of migrant lesbians also appears under rubrics other than migration, diaspora, or transnationalism. For example, Oliva Espín (1997) has insistently centered and theorized Latina migrant lesbian lives in the field of psychology. Katie Acosta's (2013) *Amigas y Amantes* theorizes "sexually nonconforming Latinas relationships with partners, families of origin, children, and friends" (2) by building on interviews that include 18 migrant women.

Information about migrant lesbians is also contained in archives and sites like *None on Record: Stories of Queer Africa*; the *LGBTQ New Americans Project* at the Brooklyn Community Pride Center; and in materials collected and created by queer migrant-serving organizations. Lesbian migrants sometimes appear on screen and in cultural productions, including plays, novels, songs, and short stories. They are often present but not marked or conceived as lesbian migrants.

Scholarship on lesbian migrants has been significantly enabled by feminist of color, queer of color, decolonial, postcolonial, and indigenous theorizing, whose richness and multiplicity defy summary but generally make expansive use of intersectionality theories. Drawing from Grace Hong and Roderick Ferguson (2015), we may say that these diverse bodies of work "provide alternative understandings of subjectivity, collectivity, and power" (2). They particularly engage questions of difference framed not as multicultural celebration that serves neoliberalism, but as produced through power and violence; as multiple, relational, and non-binary; and as tied to processes of valuing and devaluing that unevenly distribute possibilities for living and dying (11, 16). The works offer diverse theoretical and methodological tools to challenge binary and linear logics; center those at the intersection of nondominant positionalities; rethink spatialities and temporalities; create ways to describe that which has been rendered unknowable and valueness (Hong and Ferguson 2015, 16); and suggest forms of consciousness and world-making practices that seek to remake the dominant order.

Scholarship on lesbian migrants is also made possible by the shift toward transnational, postcolonial, decolonial, hemispheric, and regional analyses of migration. These approaches resituate nations and states within global histories of empire and capitalism that continually drive migration. The theories denaturalize hegemonic nationalist and statist frameworks that legitimize yet erase histories of violence and dispossession that underpin immigration policies. For example, Alyosha Goldstein (2014) describes, "the United States encompasses a historically variable and uneven constellation of state and local governments, indigenous nations, unincorporated territories, free associated commonwealths, protectorates, federally administered public lands, military bases, export processing zones, colonias, and anomalies such as the District of Colombia... the heterogeneity of this condition is not exceptional to the United States" (1). This heterogeneity reflects multiple processes of violence and dispossession that underpin, and continually threaten to rupture, hegemonic assertions of nationhood, statehood, and sovereignty; at the same time, these hegemonic assertions legitimize policies and practices that render migrants exploitable and disposable. From within transnational, postcolonial, hemispheric, and regional frameworks, migrants are conceived not within binary and linear logics that posit leaving one bounded nation-state for another or shedding one set of cultural norms for another, but as people whose migration was shaped by political, economic, and cultural flows across centuries and borders; as embedded in ongoing relationships that span national borders; and as navigating colonial, capitalist, racial, gender, and sexual hegemonies at different scales.

Borders and borderlands scholarship have also been critical by reconceiving borders not as self-evident lines on a map, but as materializations of histories of power and struggle that are tied to broad economic, social, and political dynamics at different scales involving multiple temporalities. Gloria Anzaldúa's (1987) pathbreaking work, which theorized the United

States/Mexico border as both metaphor and material site, has inspired dense explorations of borders as sites of power, inequality, struggle, dispossession, and world-making. Centering working-class, lesbian of color, border-dweller experiences and consciousness, Anzaldúa offered methods that refuse binary logics in favor of multiple, relational, and decolonial approaches. Scholars underscore that migration, and state strategies for governing migrants, continually challenge and reconstitute the nature and function of borders, including in the present moment.

The tools offered by affect theory are also increasingly used to theorize migrant lives, including those of lesbians.[4] Migration scholarship has consistently engaged with feelings of love, loss, belonging, attachment, and desire that are associated with migration experiences (e.g., Mai and King 2009). Recent affect theories enable scholars to interconnect migrant subjectivities to structural dynamics in new ways, exploring relays of power and transformation. For instance, Jørgen Carling and Francis Collins (2018) use affect theory to rethink hegemonic explanations for why migration occurs. Explanations have remained polarized between those frameworks centered on imaginaries of sovereign individuals who make rational, calculated migration decisions, yet without addressing structural barriers, and frameworks that conceive migration as an outcome of histories and dynamics of colonialism and capitalism, yet without accounting for people's agency. Using affect theory as a bridge, Carling and Collins argue that desire and aspiration, which are co-produced individually and socially, interact with the structural drivers of migration in a continually unfolding process that often defies linear logics and state-centric perspectives. Moreover, they argue that migration is not an end in itself, but a process through which people seek to *become* or to achieve aspirations, which may change over time.[5]

Recent work especially builds from Sara Ahmed's (2010) insight that affect is not contained within individuals, but instead circulates among people and objects, materializing them in ways that build on historic inequalities and modes of dispossession, yet opening up possibilities for transformation. Accordingly, scholars have debated the connections between affective investments in Whiteness, carcerality, and empire on one hand, and increasingly exclusionary and punitive immigration policies on the other; and whether and how such affective investments can be extended, short-circuited, or routed elsewhere. Conversely, they consider possibilities and limits of investments in frameworks such as global human rights and cosmopolitan citizenship. These debates are deeply in dialogue with scholarship on affective citizenship that, as Fortier (2016, 1038) describes, understands citizenship not only or primarily as juridical status, a regime of rights, and/or belonging, but as an object to which affects attach and are struggled over, in ways that continually remake and re-stratify citizenship. Possibilities for rethinking affect theory in conjunction with queer women of color theory, which are directly relevant to this special issue, were the focus of a special issue of the *Journal of Lesbian Studies* that was edited by Aimee Carrillo Rowe and Francesca T. Royster (2017).

Recent book-length studies from the growing field of trans or transgender studies also offer tools that promise to transform how we conceive lesbian migrant lives. Trans studies have valuably challenged the assumption that gender concerns social roles or norms whereas sex concerns nature or biology; instead, trans studies insist that both genders and sexes are complexly constituted and disassembled, do not fall into binaries, and do not necessarily align with one another or into normative gender categories. The analytic promises to transform how scholars analyze gender as a category that shapes and becomes reshaped by migration—especially as the voices and experiences of trans migrants, including lesbian-identified trans migrants, become incorporated into and transform migration knowledge.

A significant strand of trans studies theorizes the interplay between technologies and embodiment; Toby Beauchamp (2019) links these works to critical surveillance studies. Dubrovsky and Magnet (2015) argue that surveillance technologies and practices "normalize and maintain whiteness, able-bodiedness, capitalism and heterosexuality, practices integral to the foundation of the modern state" (7); Beauchamp's work suggests connections between looking, tracking, surveillance, embodiment, and state-making that are vital to understanding migrant lesbian lives.

The growing scholarship linking prison with border abolition (e.g., Loyd et al. 2013) and on detention, deportation, and making migrants "illegal" (e.g. Lewis 2013; Luibhéid and Chávez forthcoming) is also directly relevant to understanding migrant lesbian lives. So is human rights scholarship which, as Lewis and Naples (2014, 911) suggest, would be strengthened by further engaging LGBTQ migration debates.

Telling and terminology

Lesbian

But who and what is a "migrant or refugee lesbian"? Omise'eke Tinsley (2010, 15) writes, "when a woman loves a woman in the Caribbean, none of these words will mean the same as they do in the Global North," or elsewhere. This special issue does not conceive "lesbian" as essential or transhistorical, but as a term whose meanings and boundaries are inseparable from processes of colonialism, capitalism, racialization, and patriarchy. The meanings and boundaries of the term are constantly being struggled over, contested, and remade, including through migration processes.

Contributors to the special issue wrestle with the term and employ other related, though not commensurate, terms, including queer, gay, nonheteronormative, bisexual, two spirit, and fluid. I use "lesbian" as a shorthand to signal these and other related terms and histories, not as an act of capture or closure.

Just like the term "lesbian" is not intended as a reference to some sort of essential, transhistorical, or transnationally unmediated identity, lesbian sexualities are not presented as essential, but as formed within the larger processes through which all sexualities are produced, governed, and transformed, including migration processes, discourses, and institutions.[6] Deniz Akin (2017) argues that sexuality, like gender, is not something that people inherently "possess," but instead an emergent feature of all social interactions, including in contexts of navigating migration systems and processes. Migrant women "do" or perform lesbian identifications in different ways in different contexts, and lesbianism (like any sexual identity, including normative heterosexuality) is a "recurring accomplishment" rather than an essential identity. Therefore, rather than seeking to identify "real" lesbians or evaluating how these migrants conform or not to various, often Eurocentric norms of lesbian identity and sexuality, the essays collected here are concerned with understanding how normalizing regimes of power seek to construct, capture, abject, stigmatize, dispossess or otherwise appropriate lesbian identified and non-heteronormative migrant women's lives and bodies. At the same time, the essays allow for the heterogeneity of women who identify as lesbian or related terms; the continually emergent nature of their identifications, practices, and dissidences; and their creative and resistant responses to demands to make themselves legible in particular ways.

The term "lesbian" refers not just to sexual, but also gender identification, and to the interaction of female sexual and gender identifications. Thus, "lesbian" marks a space for the intersection for several non-dominant identities, which, following Crenshaw, contributes to resistance to their telling in migration and related scholarship. Like sexuality, gender identifications are constructed, policed, inhabited, and rearticulated within multiple relations of power. African/diaspora and Indigenous studies feminist scholarship especially alerts us to the ways that gender ordering stems from and secures racial and colonial logics and histories, including genocide, dispossession, and slavery. Trans studies scholarship, especially work that centers African American (Snorton 2017) and Indigenous histories (McMullin 2011), has further elaborated the complexities of gender in ways that promise to transform migration scholarship. Taking note of these important works, this special issue centers lesbian migrants in a manner that interconnects lesbian (queer/nonheteronormative) sexuality and female gender. It also understands lesbians as women loving women who may also have male lovers, be or have been married to men, have children, be sex workers, be sexually exploited, be dominatrices, and much more. It understands female gender in non-reductive, non-binary, and trans inclusive ways that take into account the importance of racialization, economics, and geopolitics as vital for the tellability of lesbian migrants' lives.

Thus, in this special issue, lesbian is an open-ended term that women variously claim and inhabit; the articles ask us to understand what that term means, what it can do, and how and why women claim and inhabit it within specific, changing contexts and histories.

Migrant and refugee

I employ the term "migrant" as a reference to anyone who has crossed an international border except for purposes of tourism. The term deliberately refuses the state's efforts to taxonomize and classify migrants through shifting categories which are used to surveil, normalize, and/or criminalize while defining associated rights and rightlessness.

"Migrant" evokes the fact that nation-states and supranational bodies have come to monopolize the control over people's migration across international borders (Torpey 2000). That system for managing international migration is relatively recent, and builds on histories of colonialism, global capitalism, racial slavery, and genocide. In the late nineteenth and early twentieth centuries, as the global order became re-scaled into one of supposedly sovereign nation-states, nation-state controls over migration built on and reproduced these historic inequalities, resulting in global apartheid.

In issuing the Call For Papers for this special issue, I called for works on migrant and refugee lesbian experiences. I used the framing of "migrant and refugee" hesitantly because I do not wish to naturalize dominant logics that differentiate between migrants (presumed to be making voluntary choices) and refugees or asylum seekers (presumed to be forced migrants). That binary denies that most migrants experience conditions of both force and choice to varying degrees; even more importantly, the binary serves states that use it to try to immobilize and criminalize a vast majority of the world's migrants, whether through economic or humanitarian logics. However, states *do* make a distinction between migrants and refugees that translates into important differences for governing and policing migrants, which are reflected in scholarship. Thus, my call for scholarship about migrant and refugee lesbians sought works that historicize and interrogate the different systems through which migrants must pass, not that reify the binary between chosen and forced migration.

The essays here focus on processes of crossing international borders (as distinct from experiences of internally displaced people, those navigating the hukou system in China,[7] or related processes). They engage the state and supranational migration regimes; they engage other scales, too. No essay, however, addresses crossing the boundaries of Indigenous nations, which are also instances of crossing international borders.

Colonialist binaries and migration narratives

Clearly, terminologies are implicated in relationships of power that mediate (im)possibilities of telling. The question of "telling" is also haunted by and entangled with colonialist binaries of out/closeted, visible/invisible, home/homeless, and victim/agent, among others, which the essays take on and complicate. For example, the dominant model of coming out conceptualizes lesbian or gay identification within a linear, progressive narrative as something that one must understand about oneself, accept, claim, and publicly share. Failure to do so is regarded as evidence of internalized repression, pathology, lack of adjustment, and inability to be a proper subject. Yet, the progress model draws from and reinscribes racializing, colonialist, and capitalist logics that normalize White, middle-class, gender-normative citizen subjects while positioning everyone else as Other or lacking. When migrants don't match the model, this is treated as evidence that they are likely to be from backwards, repressive, or quaintly/touristically "different" cultures and communities that need to "catch up"—rather than that the model is fatally Eurocentric. The model has become harnessed to forms of neoliberal governmentality that frame the effects of inequality as personal rather than systemic problems (Clare 2017; Decena 2011, 18–19).

The closeted/coming out narrative connects with binaries such as speech/silence and visible/invisible that scholarship has contested, and that essays here further extend. For example, Carlos Decena's research shows that Dominican migrant gay men in New York City generally did not explain or announce their sexual identities, but "were not silent about it" (19), either. Theorizing the men as "tacit subjects," Decena argues that what is tacit is neither silent nor secret (19), and that operating as tacit subjects whose sexuality was widely known but not discussed enabled access to social networks and resources that were crucial for survival and, in some cases, advancement.

Questions of silence and speech thoroughly interconnect with the contested politics of visibility, invisibility, and hypervisibility (which in turn connect to questions about the possibilities and limits of seeking recognition and rights from states and corporations). Susana Peña (2013) brings a gendered analysis to the interplay between silence, in/visibility and hypervisibility, arguing that whereas gay men "in Cuban and Cuban American contexts have had to contend with a stigmatizing hypervisibility, lesbians in these same contexts have had to face cultural unintelligibility" (xxvii). Her book analyzes how Cuban gay/queer migrant men navigated contradictory, changing regimes of silence, in/visibility, and hypervisibility as they sought to create spaces of possibility in the context of racial, gender, and class dynamics that shaped their migration from Cuba to Miami, Florida. How Cuban lesbians navigated these regimes is suggested by scattered articles. Francesca Stella (2012) has retheorized visibility/invisibility in regard to place- and space-making. Centering the Russian city of Ul'yanovsk, where queers/lesbians appropriated public spaces for socializing and hanging out, Stella argues that invisibility was "an expression of both accommodation and resistance to existing social norms. Resistance was expressed not through visibility, rarely considered empowering or desirable, but through collective action, which produced fluid boundaries between the tusovka [social network] and the outside world, and allowed the articulation of shared identities and experiences within these boundaries" (1843). Aren Aizura extends these debates by advocating for a politics of exodus that is "not visible but disidentifying and invisible in the spectacular economies of representation and calculability inhabited by both non-government organizations and the state" (150). Such a politics refuses "an easy dialectic between recognition and misrecognition, visibility and invisibility, or discipline and escape" (150).

Scholars have significantly reworked constructions of home and belonging in order to provide better tools for conceptualizing migrant lesbian lives. Gayatri Gopinath (2005) describes that dominant conceptions of "home" depend on gendered, patriarchal, and spatializing logics that are also central to normative notions of race, nation, and diaspora; in this context, the lesbian can only exist as an impossible subject who is positioned as "outside" (18). Gopinath theorizes queer diasporic cultural forms that "redefine home outside a logic of blood, purity, authenticity, and patrilineal descent" (187) and allow for lesbian existence (see also Fortier 2001, 2002).

Several essays in the special issue further extend these discussions on silence/speech, invisibility/visibility/hypervisibility, and homelessness/home. They contend with the fact that lesbians' migration is often either completely ignored or else narrated within the colonialist binaries described earlier. Either approach affirms and naturalizes hegemonic imaginaries of bounded nation-states and citizenries, even though these frameworks are becoming "increasingly fractured and shaky" (Allen et al. 2017, 218) in the context of neoliberalism and globalization. Hilka Amit's (2018) study of queer Israeli emigrants provides an example of how lesbian and queer migrants get ignored. According to Amit, the standard emigration narrative, which is widely used by Israeli politicians, academics, and media, asserts that "the emigrants leave to improve their economic situation, that they wish to return to Israel, and that they feel a great connection to Israeli society and the state" (45). Amit's queer interviewees (of whom 19 identified as women) made clear that these frameworks did not reflect their experiences or reasons for migrating, which, according to Amit, involve an implicit critique of the state and dominant national culture.[8] Even after departure, their relation to Israel remained "critical rather than nostalgic" (38). Since dominant emigration narratives serve state- and nation-making, there was and is no space to represent these critical, queer emigrant lives. When not shrouded in silence, queer migration may be represented as an exodus by "deviants" who are unduly influenced by "foreign" values and cultures.

From the "immigration" perspective of nation-states in which migrants arrive, LGBTQ migration, when it is addressed rather than ignored, tends to be framed using linear, binary, and colonialist models of movement "from repression to liberation," or what I have elsewhere described as "liberationist narratives" (Luibhéid 2005, xxv). The framework serves dominant state and national logics by constructing migrants as backward and repressed; erases their internal difference; and ignores the ways that globalization has reconfigured sexualities within migrants' own countries (Cantú 2009, 76–80). That framework further ignores interconnections among nation-states that contribute to migration; essentializes sexuality while cutting it off from the multiple dynamics that generate migration; ranks nation states; and erases the reality of violence within "destination" countries. It fuels the enduring trope of migrant communities (and marginalized communities within nation-states) as deeply homophobic and repressive or deviant, depending on the context. As the essays collected here show, this logic also authorizes state inquiry into migrants' lives and being and affirms the supposed queer-friendliness and wonderfulness of the nation-state to which people migrate, and its generous, welcoming, open-minded citizens (Raboin 2017).

Silencing, or forms of telling that silence, shows up in ways other than dominant narratives that states and citizenries construct about migrants. For example, in order to be able to migrate, people must navigate regimes of telling and concealing. Historically, states have banned immigration by lesbians and other "deviants" who were deemed to threaten the reproduction of the nation; even without an explicit ban, legal admission has remained difficult or impossible; and these im/possibilities connected to documentary and other requirements that constitute forms of telling and concealing that are mandated by states as well as by social, cultural, and economic networks. Possibilities for entry, remaining, transitioning from insecure to secure status, and maintaining ties to families, communities, and resources depended on becoming fluent in the different forms of telling and concealing that were expected at various junctures, as well as developing strategies for responding without jeopardizing social, economic, and other capital. Melissa Autumn White (2014) suggests that migration documents function not only as mandated forms of telling, but also as "transference machines of emotion" (88) that "materialize a profoundly affective encounter between migrants and state bureaucrats" (77), impacting the disposition of migration cases. Demands for telling have also shifted as same-sex marriage becomes a ground for legal immigration in growing numbers of countries.

Refugee and asylum systems have come to demand extensive forms of telling, including about one's sexuality. The refugee/asylum system is rooted in the 1951 Geneva Convention and the 1967 Protocol Relating to the Status of Refugees, which provide possibilities for refugee or asylum status to those who can show that they have experienced persecution, or fear future persecution, on one of five grounds. The grounds are race, religion, nationality, political opinion, or membership in a particular social group.[9] After significant struggle, lesbian, gay, and trans identities became recognized by some two dozen nation-states as constituting "membership in a particular social group" for which individuals might be persecuted, and therefore as grounds for seeking asylum.

Gaining refugee or asylum status on the basis of lesbian identity hinges on proving that one *is* a lesbian and faces the risk of persecution as a result. Credibility, immutability of identity, and past or likely future persecution are key elements of successful claims, all of which require specific ways of "telling." Much has been written about demands placed on asylum-seeking migrants to narrate their experiences in ways that fit ethnocentric and essentialist understandings of sexual identities that stem from and reproduce racist and colonialist logics, and how those processes serve hegemonic state-, nation-, and citizenship-building processes while rarely assisting migrants (e.g., Murray 2015; Raboin 2017). For example, Thibault Raboin (2017) argues that, in the UK, narratives of asylum offer a means to stage the British state and nation as queer positive (17) and the British public as liberal subjects who are moved by spectacles of suffering and who desire for "the right thing" to be done (29), even while asylum seekers continue to be deported. These logics implicate others in addition to states and citizens:

> ... pro bono legal and specialist NGOs frequently (re)articulate, enact, and extend limited and limiting governmental logics and hegemonic discourses concerning LGBT asylum seekers. Their investments in homonormative, Western-informed ideas about LGBT subjectivity—particularly that sexuality is immutable, and that coming

out is both necessary and inevitable—function simultaneously to regulate individuals seeking asylum, to reaffirm the expectations of [immigration] officers adjudicating asylum claims, and to reassert homonationalist imaginaries. (McGuirk 2018, 16–17)

The particular difficulties facing lesbian-identified women within these configurations of power have received some attention. Rachel Lewis (2013) suggests that the very idea of lesbian sexuality remains significantly inconceivable to adjudicators and publics (and often has to be established through forms of telling that migrant women experience as demeaning, pornographic, invasive, and violent). Women who have been married to men, have a child, are feminine or femme-presenting, or cannot point to sexual experiences with other women and/or direct participation in normative gay culture face particular difficulties. These difficulties reflect that the asylum system is unable to conceptualize and address what Schuman and Bohmer (2014) describe as "confounding vulnerabilities"; in other words, the intersection of gender with sexuality (and class, racialization, and geopolitics) in shaping experiences leading up to asylum claims. Crenshaw's formulation of people in this situation as having "lives that resist telling," yet as being targets for state and non-state violence, speaks to this predicament.

Deniz Akin suggests that the women learn and mobilize strategies to "translate" their experiences into the language that courts demand, showing that they are not passive victims even though they're expected to narrate themselves as such. In some cases, as Rachel Lewis shows, women whose claims of lesbian identity are disbelieved during the asylum process strategically deploy social media to publicize their lesbian identifications, thereby seeking to preempt government efforts to deport them. Women also develop new ways of telling their lives on their own terms through cultural work and participation in organizations. At the same time, as David A. B. Murray describes, asylum processes demand that migrants engage in homonationalist identifications and performances. Within migrant communities, some become judges of others' sexualities, problematically echoing the ways that immigration systems and NGOs function as arbiters of "real" and not real sexual identities.

Even as asylum seekers develop strategies for "telling" in ways that are legible for adjudicators, NGOs, and others, they often find it necessary to conceal, hide, or not tell their sexualities and identifications in miserable asylum seeker accommodations, on the streets, and in workplaces and public venues. Sima Shakhsari (2014) underlines the irony of Iranian asylum seekers in Turkey who the United Nations High Commissioner for Refugees (UNHCR) deems to have "passed" the interviews required to "prove" their lesbian sexualities and therefore their eligibility to be considered for asylum, yet while in public, work and other spaces, they must "pass" as sexually and gender normative (1006). Shakhsari observes, "Passing the test of being gay, lesbian or transgender according to the UNHCR standards, and passing as straight or cisgender at work or in public in Turkey mark forms of policing and surveillance that queer and trans refugees experience on a daily basis" (1006).

These processes reveal some of the relations of power that mediate processes of "telling" in ways that are struggled over, and serve diverse interests, although rarely the priorities of asylum-seeking women. Akin suggests that the fact that asylum seekers develop strategies to translate and tell about their sexualities in ways that are legible to adjudicators, and that sometimes result in legal status, does not subvert but instead affirms the dominant system, including the right of supranational bodies and states to control people's migration in ways that criminalizes and dispossesses millions. Some scholars advocate for more "culturally sensitive" models for assessing lesbian asylum claims. Others suggest that since the asylum system primarily involves what Bohmer and Schuman (2007) call "epistemologies of ignorance" that legitimize violence, detention and deportation, the abolition of all migration regimes offers the only long-term solution.

Essays in the special issue

The essays gathered here are not intended to be "representative" of regions or scholarly fields, which would be impossible, but instead reflect responses to the CFP's circulation and engagement in specific contexts and historical moments. The essays neither promise nor provide any transparent telling, but instead interrogate the power relations that structure im/possibilities of telling. They all grapple with tellability in regard to lives that exist at the intersection of multiple, non-majority identities—not in the sense of identity as an unchanging personal possession or essential quality, but as a positionality within social, economic, cultural, and political relations. The essays avoid telling about migrant lesbian lives in universalizing ways and instead analyze specific histories, contexts, and configurations of power. They piece together varied social science methodologies and theories, while pushing at their limits. The essays show the diversity of women's migration circumstances and available resources, thereby challenging singular and homogenizing narratives of migrants and migration. They capture how state migration regimes in conjunction with multiple institutions of power seek to subjectify and govern migrant lesbians in often contradictory ways, and how migrant lesbians cope, strategize, and respond to these structural conditions. In the process, the essays complicate and rework binaries of visibility/invisibility, in/out, victim/agent, home/homeless, belonging/unbelonging. Tellability as such emerges as a technology of power and violence, and conversely, as a mode of healing, (re)building a sense of self and connection to others, and creating conditions for what several authors describe as livability and queer world making. Collectively, the essays raise critical questions about the political, ethical, and epistemological stakes of telling; who gets to tell, when, and under what conditions; when, whether, and how telling may shift relations of power and inequality; and the ways in which tellability is implicated in sanctioning or challenging forms of violence that make migrant lesbian women disposable.

Eddie Alvarez centers the silence in scholarship about the lives of everyday, working-class Latina lesbian migrants in Los Angeles who are forging lives in the midst of struggle. Employing an innovative framework that he calls "finding sequins in the rubble," Alvarez explores themes of migration, leisure space, and family in the lives of two lesbians, one from Mexico and the other from Guatemala, who live in Los Angeles. Alvarez's methodology seeks to enable the women to tell their lives on their own terms, showing how they engage in processes of "queer-world making and radical possibility through everyday acts of resilience and self-care in the midst of familial, institutional, and state violence."

Sandibel Borges also employs oral history to gather information about the lives of five LGBTQ Latina migrant women who experience a constant struggle to survive in the face of systemic violence and dehumanization. Borges explores how the women, who are currently based on Los Angeles and Mexico City, engage in resistance through survival, community building, and activism. She argues that resistance fosters healing, which further enables resistance, in a process that is never solely individual but also collective. These dynamics "contradict the isolation, displacement and social abandonment created by systems of migration, heteronormativity, and White supremacy." Through resistance and healing, the women imagine and create livable lives at multiple scales.

Mia Liinason's chapter explores livability in the lives of non-heterosexual migrant Muslim women in Norway and Denmark. Her fieldwork with two LGBTI organizations provided insight about the limitations of the "Western visibility paradigm" for understanding these migrant lesbians' lives. Liinason argues that the women are "involved in multi-layered negotiations" in relation to their families, homes, queer communities, and nations. Seeking to move away from binary logics of in/out or visible/invisible that are thoroughly implicated in homotolerence, Islamophobia and homophobia, and from essentialist models of identity and place, Liinason argues that the women's positioning "could be interpreted as simultaneously in and out of the closet or, neither in nor out." Liinason concludes that attention to "conditions and relations that make lives livable" offers the most helpful and respectful framework for analysis.

Lucetta Kam's essay centers on *chuguo*, or going abroad, which has become widely regarded as a desirable means for getting ahead in post-reform China. Focusing on a group of relatively privileged lesbian or *lala* women who migrated from major Chinese urban areas to Australia, Kam shows how *chuguo* allows them to navigate heteronormative gender and sexual demands from families, communities, and mainstream society while nonetheless pursuing their own aspirations and dreams. Kam concludes that transnational mobility has become a new homonormative value that reflects changing cultural and structural logics in post-reform China.

Elif Sarı draws from fieldwork to critically explore how Iranian lesbian asylum seekers navigate the different, often contradictory demands for telling about their bodies, identities, and sexualities that get placed on them by asylum, welfare, and humanitarian regimes in Turkey. As Sarı argues, all of these different actors are actively involved in producing, interpreting, assessing, making real or inauthentic, making deserving or undeserving, "lesbian" identities based on particular tropes. Asylum-seeking women must negotiate and perform identities and sexualities in these varied contexts in order to access vital supports, resources, and possibilities. Sarı concludes that these processes of "making up people" not only affect lesbian asylum seekers' present and future possibilities, but also transform how they imagine and embody their own genders and sexualities, and interpret others'.

Conclusion

How to create conditions for telling that challenge rather than normalize violent logics of capitalist, state, nation, and citizenship building? When and how can academic work, which often serves dominant relations, instead contribute to transformative forms of telling? What other modes of telling can be fostered and further supported? An inspiring example is offered by *None on Record*, formed by Selly Thiam after activist FannyAnn Eddy from Sierra Leone was murdered. *None on Record* began as an oral history project that collected over 350 stories of LGBT Africans, including LGBT Africans who migrated within their countries, across the African continent, and from the continent. Over time, *None on Record* became "a digital media organization that produces multimedia documentaries and teaches digital media skills in African LGBT communities" (https://www.noneonrecord.com). The work of telling stories of African LGBT people, both migrant and nonmigrant, has expanded and changed form as more people became involved; as organizers have offered tailored trainings and technologies; and as arts festival and regular podcasts were created and circulated. According to *None On Record*'s website, trainings take place under conditions that are attentive to security concerns of participants and trainers. *None on Record* also opened an East Africa office "to challenge the narratives around LGBT experiences. This work is critical on the African continent where local media ignores or vilifies LGBT communities and foreign reporting creates an image of LGBT people as passive victims of homophobic acts and policies." The *None on Record* project reveals complex intersections of power and struggle that shape im/possibilities for telling; the urgencies and joys of telling for those living at the intersections of multiple, nondominant positionalities; and how processes of telling contribute to changing the conditions among migrants and nonmigrants alike.

Taking inspiration from work like that of *None On Record* and many others, the essays in this special issue lay significant groundwork to enable transformative forms of telling, while making clear the stakes. They highlight forms of telling that center the intersections of sexualities and genders in contexts of racial, cultural, capitalist, and colonialist violence. Read alongside Crenshaw, the essays suggest the urgency of fostering forms of telling that enable those living at the intersections of multiple, non-dominant positionalities to speak about their experiences, thereby forcing an accounting of power that challenges the structural devaluation and sanctioned erasure of some lives (Hong and Ferguson 2015). They inspire us to demand changes that foster livable and dignified lives for all.

Notes

1. Loyd, Mitchelson and Burridge (2013) speak of the urgency of developing "organizing strategies that don't depend on winning one set of (apparent) privileges through reinforcing someone else's oppression" (9).
2. This review of scholarship is intended to be illustrative rather than exhaustive, since the conversations span so many disciplines and locations.
3. See also the invaluable collection of Alexander's essays (2005).
4. I follow Fortier by using affect to "designate a generic category of emotions and feelings including embodied and sensory feelings through which we experience the world, and through which worlds, subjects, and objects are brought forth" (2016, 1039).
5. Sexual/gender identifications (by everyone, including lesbians) can be understood as involving desires and aspirations that are unfolding but never fully accomplished; and that interact with migration systems and processes in continually evolving ways. These desires and aspirations are neither reducible to nor separate from drivers of migration that include capitalism, colonialism, and military interventions.
6. However, those who seem to approximate dominant sexuality logics enjoy the benefit of having their beings and records less subject to scrutiny and doubt; contrarily, those who do not match are continually asked to prove and explain their sexualities and beings.
7. For a brief explanation of the hukou system, see https://projectpartner.org/poverty/hukou-system-explained-chinas-internal-passport/

8. Amit's study is based on interviews with 42 people, of whom 19 identified as women, 22 identified as men, and one identified as F2M (xvi).
9. See https://www.unhcr.org/lgbti-claims.html.

Acknowledgments

Warmest thanks to Esther Rothblum for inviting this special issue and her guidance throughout the process; Karma Chávez and Annie Hill for practical and insightful suggestions that greatly improved the introduction; and the Latino Research Initiative for a generous fellowship during which this special issue was completed.

References

Acosta, Katie. *Amigas y Amantes: Sexually Nonconforming Latinas Negotiate Family*. New Brunswick, NJ: Rutgers University Press, 2013.

Ahmed, Sara. *The Promise of Happiness*. Durham, NC: Duke University Press, 2010.

Aizura, Aren. "Transnational Transgender Rights and Immigration Law." In *Transfeminist Perspectives in and Beyond Transgender and Gender Studies*, ed. Finn Enke, 133–150. Philadelphia, PA: Temple University Press, 2012.

Aizura, Aren. *Mobile Subjects: Transnational Imaginaries of Gender Reassignment*. Durham, NC: Duke University Press, 2018.

Akin, Deniz. "Queer Asylum Seekers: Translating Sexuality in Norway," *Journal of Ethnic and Migration Studies 43*, no. 3 (2017): 458–474.

Alexander, Jacqui M. "Not Just Any Body Can Be a Citizen: The Politics of Law, Sexuality and Postcolonialist in Trinidad and Tobago and the Bahamas," *Feminist Review 48* (Autumn 1994): 5–23.

Alexander, Jacqui M. *Pedagogies of Crossing: Meditations on Feminism, Sexual Politics, Memory, and the Sacred*. Durham, NC: Duke University Press, 2005.

Amit, Hila. *A Queer Way Out: The Politics of Queer Emigration from Israel*. Albany, NY: State University of New York Press, 2018.

Allen, William et al. "Who Counts in a Crisis? The New Geopolitics of International Migration and Refugee Governance," *Geopolitics 23*, no. 1 (2017): 217–243.

Anzaldúa, Gloria. *Borderlands/La Frontera: The New Mestiza*. San Francisco, CA: Aunt Lute, 1987.

Beauchamp, Toby. *Going Stealth: Transgender Politics and US Surveillance Practices*. Durham, NC: Duke University Press, 2019.

Bohmer, Carol and Amy Schuman. "Producing Epistemologies of Ignorance in the Political Asylum Process," *Identities: Global Studies in Culture and Power 14* (2007): 603–629.

Cantú, Lionel Jr.. *The Sexuality of Migration: Border Crossings and Mexican Immigrant Men*, eds. Nancy A. Naples and Salvador Vidal-Ortiz. New York, NY: New York University Press, 2009.

Carling, Jørgen and Francis Collins. "Aspiration, Desire, and Drivers of Migration," *Journal of Ethnic and Migration Studies 44*, no. 6 (2018): 909–926.

Chávez, Karma R.. *Queer Migration Politics: Activist Rhetoric and Coalitional Possibilities*. Urbana, IL: University of Illinois Press, 2013.

Clare, Stephanie. "'Finally, She's Accepted Herself!' Coming Out in Neoliberal Times," *Social Text 131 35*, no. 2 (June 2017): 17–38.

Crenshaw, Kimberlé. "Whose Story is it Anyway? Feminist and Antiracist Appropriations of Anita Hill," in *Race-ing Justice, Engendering Power: Essays on Anita Hill, Clarence Thomas, and the Construction of Social Reality*, ed. Toni Morrison. New York, NY: Pantheon Books, 1992), 402–440.

Decena, Carlos Ulises. *Tacit Subjects: Belonging and Same-Sex Desire among Dominican Immigrant Men*. Durham, NC: Duke University Press, 2011.

Dubrovsky, Rachel and Shoshana Amielle Magnet. "Introduction: Feminist Surveillance Studies: Critical Interventions," in *Feminist Surveillance Studies*, eds. Rachel Dubrovsky and Shoshana Amielle Magnet. Durham, NC: Duke University Press, 2015), 1–17.

El-Tayeb, Fatima. *European Others: Queering Ethnicity in Postnational Europe*. Minneapolis, MN: University of Minnesota Press, 2011.

Espín, Oliva. *Latina Realities: Essays on Healing, Migration and Sexuality*. New York, NY: Routledge, 1997.

Fortier, Anne-Marie. "'Coming Home': Queer Migrations and Multiple Evocations of Home," *European Journal of Cultural Studies 4*, no. 4 (2001): 405–424.

Fortier, Anne-Marie. "Queer Diaspora," in *Handbook of Lesbian and Gay Studies*, eds. Diane Richardson and Steven Seidman. Thousand Oaks, CA: Sage, 2002), 183–197.

Fortier, Anne-Marie. "Afterword: Acts of Affective Citizenship? Possibilities and Limitations," *Citizenship Studies 20*, no. 8 (2016): 1038–1044.

Giametta, Calogero. *The Sexual Politics of Asylum: Sexual Orientation and Gender Identity*. New York, NY: Routledge, 2017.

Goldstein, Alyosha. "Introduction: Toward a Genealogy of the U.S. Colonial Present," in *Formations of United States Colonialism*, ed. Alyosha Goldstein. Durham, NC: Duke University Press, 2014), 1–30.

Gopinath, Gayatri. *Impossible Desires: Queer Diasporas and South Asian Public Cultures*. Durham, NC: Duke University Press, 2005.

Hong, Kyungwon Grace and Roderick Ferguson. "Introduction," in *Strange Affinities: The Gender and Sexual Politics of Comparative Racialization*, eds. Grace Kyungwon Hong and Roderick Ferguson. Durham, NC: Duke University Press, 2015), 1–22.

Kuntsman, Adi. *Figurations of Violence and Belonging: Queerness, Migranthood and Nationalism in Cyberspace and Beyond*. Oxford, England: Peter Lang, 2009.

Lai, Francisca Yuenki. "Migrant and Lesbian Activism in Hong Kong: A Critical Review of Grassroots Politics," *Asian Anthropology 17*, no. 2 (2018): 135–150.

Lewis, Rachel. "Deportable Subjects: Lesbians and Political Asylum," *Feminist Formations 25* no. 2 (Summer 2013): 174–194.

Lewis, Rachel and Nancy Naples. "Introduction: Queer Migration, Asylum, and Displacement," *Sexualities 17*, no. 8 (2014): 911–918.

Loyd, Jenna M., Matt Mitchelson, and Andrew Burridge, eds. *Beyond Walls and Cages*. Athens, GA: University of Georgia Press, 2013.

Luibhéid, Eithne. "Introduction," in *Queer Migrations: Sexuality, US Citizenship, and Border Crossing*, eds. Eithne Luibhéid and Lionel Cantú, Jr. Minneapolis, MN: University of Minnesota Press, 2005, ix–xlvi.

Luibhéid, Eithne and Karma R. Chávez. *Queer and Trans Migrations: Illegalization, Detention, and Deportation*. Champaign, IL: University of Illinois Press, forthcoming.

Mai, Nicola and Russell King. "Introduction: Love, Sexuality and Migration: Mapping the Issues," *Mobilities 4*, no. 3 (November 2009): 295–307.

McGuirk, Siobhan. "(In)Credible Subjects: NGOs, Attorneys, and Permissible Asylum Seeker Identities," *Political and Legal Anthropology Review 41* (2018): 4–18.

McMullin, Dan Taulapapa. "Fa'fafafine Notes: On Tagaloa, Jesus and Nafunua," in *Queer Indigenous Studies*, eds. Qwo-Li Driskill, Chris Finley, Brian Joseph Gilley, and Scott Lauria Morgensen, 81–94. Tucson, AZ: University of Arizona Press, 2011.

Muñoz, Lorena. "Entangled Sidewalks: Queer Street Vendors in Los Angeles," *The Professional Geographer 68*, no. 2 (2016): 302–308.

Murray, David A. B.. *Real Queer? Sexual Orientation and Gender Identity Refugees in the Canadian Refugee Apparatus*. Lanham, MD: Rowman and Littlefield, 2015.

Peña, Susana. *¡Oye Loca! From the Mariel Boatlift to Gay Cuban Miami*. Minneapolis, MN: University of Minnesota Press, 2013.

Raboin, Thibaut. *Discourses of Queer Asylum in the UK: Constructing a Queer Haven*. Manchester, England: Manchester University Press, 2017.

Rand, Erica. *The Ellis Island Snow Globe*. Durham, NC: Duke University Press, 2005.

Rowe, Aimee Carrillo and Francesca T. Royster, eds. "Loving Transgressions: Queer of Color Bodies, Affective Ties, Transformative Community," *Journal of Lesbian Studies 21*, no. 3 (2017): 243–369.

Schuman, Amy and Carol Bohmer. "Gender and Cultural Silences in the Political Asylum Process," *Sexualities 17*, no. 8 (December 2014): 939–957.

Shakhsari, Sima. "The Queer Time of Death: Temporality, Geopolitics, and Refugee Rights," *Sexualities 17*, no. 8 (2014), 998–1015.

Snorton, Riley. *Black on Both Sides: A History of Trans Identity*. Durham, NC: Duke University Press, 2017.

Stella, Francesca. "The Politics of In/Visibility: Carving Out Queer Space in Ul'yanovsk," *Europe-Asia Studies 64*, no. 10 (December 2012): 1822–1846

Tinsley, Omise'eke Natasha. *Thiefing Sugar: Eroticism between Women in Caribbean Literature*. Durham, NC: Duke University Press, 2010.

Torpey, John. *The Invention of the Passport*. Cambridge, England: Cambridge University Press, 2000.

Wekker, Gloria. *The Politics of Passion: Women's Sexual Culture in the Afro-Surinamese Diaspora*. New York, NY: Columbia University Press, 2006.

White, Melissa Autumn. "Archives of Intimacy and Trauma: Queer Migration Documents as Technologies of Affect," *Radical History Review 120* (Fall 2014): 75–93.

Finding sequins in the rubble: The journeys of two Latina migrant lesbians in Los Angeles

Eddy Francisco Alvarez, Jr.

ABSTRACT
Mainstream research on lesbian, gay, bisexual, transgender Los Angeles (LA) has ignored Latinx queer communities until recently, and lesbian Latinas, particularly those who are migrants and/or refugees, have been especially marginalized. Building on scholarship and creative work by Chicana, Latina, women of color feminist, queer of color, and queer migration activists and scholars, this essay contributes to research on Mexican, Central American, and Latina lesbians in LA. In her research on sexually non-conforming Latinas, Katie L. Acosta argues that to better understand Latinas' sexualities in all their complexities, future scholarly work should address the pleasures and desires of Latina lesbians, as well as the quality and stability of the relationships they nurture in the borderlands. Building on queer migration research and using what Nan Alamilla Boyd and Horacio Roque Ramírez call "queer oral history," this article focuses on two everyday lesbians in LA whose stories add depth to our understandings of LA queer history and to the lives of queer migrants in the city. The narratives of Luna and Dulce, migrant lesbians from Mexico and Guatemala, respectively, provide a context for better understanding diverse experiences of migrant Latina lesbians in LA. Situating their lives within ongoing research on lesbian Latinas, this essay focuses on three themes—migration, leisure spaces, and family—to explore how these inform the women's everyday choices and shape their practices of freedom. Their stories and perspectives have been instrumental in enabling me to develop an interdisciplinary theoretical framework that I call "finding sequins in the rubble," through which we can recognize and understand how queer Latinx communities engage in processes of queer-world making and radical possibility through everyday acts of resilience and self-care in the midst of familial, institutional, and state violence.

Introduction

In this essay, I draw from a series of queer oral history interviews conducted with two women over a period of seven years in order to note similarities but also heterogeneity among Latina migrants living in LA.

These migrant lesbians resist erasure in a national context whose policies render their complex migration journeys illegible. The narrators participated in an oral history project on queer Latinx LA during which I interviewed over thirty queer Latinx people, migrants and U.S.-born, who were living or had lived in LA, and whom I met via snowball sample technique (Goodman 1961; Alvarez 2016). Latinx refers to people of Latin American descent in the United States. The "x" is used to be inclusive of non-binary, queer, gender and sexual identities (Torres 2018). Latinx people have endured a distinct history of racialization in the United States.

Born in 1962 in Guanajuato, Mexico, Luna (pseudonym) lived in Boyle Heights, a neighborhood on the east side of LA, since 2004. Prior to that, she had been migrating back and forth across the border since the 1980s. I interviewed Luna, who identifies as a lesbian and is masculine-presenting or butch, for the first time in 2012 and then again in 2013. Our interviews were conducted solely in Spanish. Although Luna worked in a cosmetics factory Monday through Friday, on the weekends she operated a home-based business, part of the informal economy. In the autumn of 2018, we connected via Facebook video. During our video interview, Luna sat outside her apartment under a tarp that usually provides shade for her weekend business of selling homemade Mexican food. As we talked, she sipped coffee from a pottery cup and ate *pan dulce*, Mexican sweet bread.

Dulce (pseudonym) was born in 1971 in Puerto Barrios, Guatemala. In 1989, seven years before the 1996 peace accords in Guatemala, she migrated to the United States as an eighteen-year-old. Dulce is a domestic worker, trained beautician, mother, and self-identified lesbian femme. Since my first interview with Dulce in August 2012, our conversations have been almost entirely conducted in English. Minutes after I arrived and before we sat to converse, she gave me a tour of her apartment, which she shared with her dog, Frida, and her twenty-year-old son. Subsequent interviews took place on Google Hangout in May 2013 and, most recently, in October 2018 while she was house-sitting for her employers.

Migrant lesbian and queer women's stories are often illegible, unknown beyond their immediate circle due to their status as immigrants, their sexuality, and other factors. If they are not activists, academics, or artists, what is the platform through which women like Dulce and Luna can tell their story and have it be heard? Dulce and Luna's narratives illustrate, in part, what Kimberlé Crenshaw calls "intersectional disempowerment" (1992, 406). Writing about Anita Hill's testimony of being sexually harassed by Supreme Court nominee Clarence Thomas, Crenshaw argues that "Hill's inability to be heard outside of the rhetorical structures within which cultural power has been organized hampered her ability to achieve recognition and support" (403). Although their circumstances are very different from

Hill's, as lesbian migrants from Latin America, Luna and Dulce are subject to "fundamental hierarchies of social power" (Crenshaw, 404); their stories, too, "resist telling" (403). Crenshaw argues that Hill was disadvantaged by the absence of available narratives to convey the reality of her experience as a Black woman to the world (404). Using a queer oral history methodology provides a lens for understanding how the experiences of lesbian migrants like Dulce and Luna "resist telling," how we can change that, and what we can learn from their stories.

This article is divided into two main sections. The first section, centered on theory and method, engages the relationship between queer oral histories and an interdisciplinary framework I characterize as "finding sequins in the rubble." Section two is divided into three themes: family, crossing borders, and leisure spaces, which map some of Luna and Dulce's memories and reflections. I describe their histories with family members and lovers, their experiences crossing borders, how their migration processes impacted them, and the role of a nightclub in their self-conceptualizations.

Method and theory: Queer oral history and finding sequins in the rubble

Nan Alamilla Boyd and Horacio N. Roque Ramirez (2009) argue that the social space of queer oral history, in which both researcher and narrator are LGBTQ-identified, enables a type of trust and with it, the possibility of producing transformative knowledge. In this context, stories are told that would otherwise remain silenced. But a shared (or adjacent) queer identity is not necessarily sufficient. For example, the women I interviewed knew that there were things they could share with me that they couldn't with others; they trusted that I would not only comprehend but be sympathetic to the linguistic, cultural, social, and highly politicized contexts within which they lived—and told—their stories. This queer oral history exchange between narrators (queer migrant Latinas from different countries, each living in LA but with their own particular migration experience and stories) and researcher (Spanish-speaking, U.S.-born, queer Latinx who grew up in Los Angeles with close family in Mexico and a transnational childhood) offers a possibility to create new knowledge about LA. The interviews reveal an ongoing process of shaping the interviewees' lives and an excitement at sharing some of the details of their journeys beyond their immediate circles. This excitement signaled that each woman knew her story was important, even though no one had asked her to share it before (Raleigh Yow 2005). In fact, Luna often said *"dejame decirte"* (let me tell you) while describing an experience or its effect on her; that is, making a point of underscoring that she was revealing what otherwise would *not* be told (or understood). The focus on the often-untold elements of everyday lives is important because we often hear about migrants' struggles with bureaucratic and governmental agencies or how they navigate the labor market, but their intimacies and quotidian practices are frequently ignored or minimized (Manalansan 2005).

Queer migrations research helps to situate Luna and Dulce's divergent geographic and political contexts and to understand the diasporic, transnational, and globalized dimension of the journeys and everyday negotiations that queer migrants like them face (Luibhéid 2002; Cantú 2009; Manalansan 2005; Chavez 2013). Research on the experiences of Mexican and Central American migrants travelling to and living in LA helps contextualize Dulce and Luna's stories (Hamilton and Stoltz Chinchilla 2001; González-López 2005; Chinchilla and Alvarado 2009; Menjívar 2011; Portillo 2012; Abrego 2014; Borges 2015; Cárdenas 2018; Ramírez 2018). Despite this critical body of work, more scholarship is needed on the everyday experiences of queer migrants, especially Central Americans such as Dulce, who still remain largely illegible. For example, Maritza Cárdenas (2018) reminds us that queer Central American narratives like Dulce's often get lost within discourses on Latinidad and queerness; often, they must "come out" as queer and as Central American. Femme presenting lesbians like Dulce are especially invisible.

The sexual, gender, and racial identity categories that are typically used in the United States are often insufficient for capturing the ways queer Latinxs and queer migrants see themselves. Identity categories and the words used to describe ourselves are contextual and in motion (Rodríguez 2003). This is evident from how Luna and Dulce's changing use of "lesbian" unfixes temporal and geographical scales. It's not uncommon for Spanish speakers to use the word *"asi,"* meaning "like that," as a euphemism for descriptors that can have negative connotations. Although Luna and Dulce each indicated to me that they are comfortable with using the term "lesbian" as a label, in practice their usage of the term differed. During our first interview, when I asked Luna if she used the term *lesbiana* to describe herself, she answered matter of factly, "*Si, no me molesta*" (Yes, I don't mind it/it doesn't bother me). However, throughout the interview she often said *"asi"* (like that), or *"que eramos asi"* (because we were like that), seeming to avoid saying the word lesbian. Six years later, Luna used the word lesbian often during our most recent interview. On the other hand, Dulce has consistently used the term lesbian to describe herself since our first conversation. She explained that she had come to identify with the term in the U.S. although she already had feelings and attractions for women when she lived in Guatemala. She also described herself as a femme. This is especially important, given the prevalent invisibility of femme Latina lesbians.

While queer oral history claims neither to provide an absolute truth nor an unmediated version of queer lives, it is a mechanism for hearing part of a story, for appreciating the relevance of everyday queer lives—in the present instance, as those lives connect to geopolitical borders and processes of structural and institutionalized forms of oppression. My conversations with Luna and Dulce, which allowed me to hear about their resilience and spirit through the memories unearthed by our queer oral interviews, were critical to my development of the conceptual rubric "finding sequins in the rubble" (Alvarez 2016). The process of voicing their stories, being witnessed and heard, collaboratively producing new knowledge, is a form of finding sequins in the rubble, of sharing the inherent value and beauty, however evanescent, in lives and experiences too often devalued.

Finding sequins in the rubble

Queer oral history activates memories that become raw data to draw from, analyze, and connect to other physical and ephemeral sources in the archive (Mills 2006, 260).[1] Because queer archives have been profoundly shaped by an epistemology of the closet and by a curating process that has been exclusionary of lives of people of color and migrants, queer oral history provides a source of new, co-constructed knowledge. The life stories shared as fragments are tiny reflections—sequins—which together form the broader fabric of queer migrant lives. While "finding sequins in the rubble" encompasses a multi-method analysis, here I focus on the role of memories, and how this method allows for theory making. Dulce and Luna's queer oral histories in particular helped me to understand finding sequins in the rubble not just as a trope, but a means to grasp how queer migrants find beauty, hope, and love in and through the reality of violence and trauma—the rubble.

Building on scholars who argue for creating new theories and metaphors from our bodies and lives, which mirror "our understanding of the world and how to critically transform it," finding sequins in the rubble is a metaphor-based lens for grasping how minoritarian subjects like Dulce and Luna make sense of their lives and work towards personal freedom (Saavedra and Nymark 2014, 255). It is an analytical lens that is attentive to the embodied experience of being queer Latinx in LA, and stems from and builds on a queer Latinx archive of knowledge located at multiple epistemological, affective and experiential locations, and which names resistive and self-making practices. These epistemologies emerge from various sites of knowledge production (nightlife, fashion, activism), a queer Latinx archive in LA comprising both physical and ephemeral contents, including memories. Most importantly, this theory emerges from embodied knowledge centered on everyday self-making, resistance, and finding beauty in the detritus of institutional and personal trauma.

My theorization of finding sequins in the rubble builds on feminists and queers of color like Chela Sandoval (1997), Martin Manalansan (2005), and José Esteban Muñoz (1999), whose theories of oppositional consciousness, disidentification, and diasporic intimacy, respectively, attend to quotidian and resistive practices of self-making. Like Chela Sandoval's "theory and method of oppositional consciousness" or "differential practice," which describe political and everyday strategies used by women color feminists as they resist oppressive structures, "finding sequins in the rubble," has rhizomatic multi-sited and multipronged origins (1998, 353). For Manalansan, the quotidian is often undertheorized. He draws from "mundane practices," the everyday "messes" of his gay Filipino migrant informants from beauty pageants and conversations in bars and homes, calling this a process of "diasporic intimacy" (2005, 148). Similarly, Muñoz describes disidentification as being "about cultural, material and psychic survival—a response to state and global power apparatuses that employ systems of racial, sexual, and national subjugation. These routinized protocols of subjugation are brutal and painful. Disidentification is about managing and negotiating historical trauma and systemic violence" (1999, 161). More importantly, "disidentifications are strategies that are called on by minoritarian subjects throughout their everyday life" and are "not only a hermeneutic but also a possibility for freedom" (179). What links these three embodied theories is how they explain the liberatory practices employed by minoritized people as they face global and local oppressive forces. All of these inform my conceptualization of "finding sequins in the rubble."

In the following, I show how the narrators/migrants navigate the systems of control and regulation which shape/impact their everyday lives. For both women, love, desire, motherhood, and pleasure offer moments in which they could express themselves, exercising freedom despite the systemic oppression, violence, dehumanization, and militarized borders each experienced. While centered on individual experiences, Dulce and Luna's narratives reveal larger historical and political forces, as well as their self-reflexivity and intentionality in the process of creating livable lives for themselves. They reflect on the everyday choices they make in the face of structural forces, their own journeys and consciousness, and the possible meanings of personal freedom for lesbian migrants like themselves.

Negotiating family

As Katie L. Acosta reminds us, family is an important part of the experiences of lesbian Latinas who continue to struggle to affirm their post-migration sexual identities while maintaining familial ties (2008, 655). In this section, I discuss how Dulce and Luna negotiated family and kinship, including motherhood and romantic relationships, as part of their personal journey to the self. Each of their reflections on family was intertwined with overcoming physical and symbolic violence.

Migration within and from Guatemala has a long history, linked to structural and political forms of violence. Dulce's experiences, which include the domestic violence she witnessed and experienced at home, reflect that history. Her experiences with violence echo Cecilia Menjívar's claim that "political violence spread throughout state structures and reached everyone in Guatemala in one way or another" (2011, 36). Gender and gendered violence are interwoven into the fabric of everyday life. The way Dulce experienced violence, congruent with Menjívar's findings, demonstrates how the institutional and structural violence at the state level is reproduced in the space of the home via family and other interpersonal relationships.

Dulce's reflections around family were suffused with a history of domestic violence that still haunts her. The violence that she and her siblings endured from their mother was a recurring theme in our interviews. The family violence was cyclical: her father beat her mother, who in turn beat the children. Dulce explained:

> She wasn't happy. She was given to my dad and my dad was beating her up all the time. I understand her coming to us like that. I always thought when you have a kid, you can't hurt him. That's what Latina mothers do [not hurt their children but protect them].[2] Why would a mother do that? Why would she beat me? I have tried to forgive her. In order for me to be the mother I am, and having a child, talking to other women has helped me understand myself. I am a resilient child. I wanted to break that chain of abuse. I started being a mother when I was twenty-four. I feel an achievement. I am being a different person than what I was taught. She hit all of us all the time, but especially beat my brother. I don't know why but she would get so mad at him. *Que tenía que ser hombre* [he had to be a man]. I think she punished him for his femininity. She was "trying to turn him into a man." I feel bad for him. He got it the worst. I didn't understand why she was so abusive when she was also such a devout Christian. But I still love her and help her however I can.

Dulce was reflective in talking about her siblings, her relationship with her mother, about wanting to be a good parent to her son who is now twenty-four years old, and about changing the cycle of violence and trauma she experienced. She spoke of her resiliency and her knowledge of self through her lesbianism. "Being a lesbian has taught me to understand myself and understand what happened to me. It helped me understand more and where my mother comes from." Dulce's words are reminiscent of Cherríe Moraga's famous 1981 essay "La Güera," in which she describes learning about her own oppression through understanding that of her mother. "I am trying to be different," Dulce says, "because of my upbringing, having communication with them [her siblings]. Spending time. Let them know that you love them. I'm always calling [my brother]. He was the most affected out of all of us. Being in each other's lives is important. Talking to my siblings and not being so judgmental." While Dulce is critical of her mother, she also understands how patriarchy and violence have affected her. Her journey is to reverse what she saw and experienced growing up, becoming a different mother than the one she experienced, which includes being there for her two siblings who are also queer, especially her brother, and letting them know that she loves them.

Family has also been integral to Luna's journey, as she has found support through her kinship network in LA, which consists of her daughter, her son-in-law, grandchildren, friends, and romantic partners. Sandibel Borges (2015, 152) argues that migrant queer people of color who are policed for not fitting into the U.S. norm of the heterosexual nation may find a valued and familiar space of support within their immediate family, and they search for a home that is inclusive of their family. For example, until recently, Luna shared an apartment with her daughter, son-in-law, grandchildren, and her former partner Lety. Although they were no longer a couple, Luna says that they provided support for one another, and she sees Lety as family. Their queer arrangements are both reflective of and resistant to mainstream queer expectations of traditional immigrant Mexican households in LA.

During our most recent conversations in the autumn of 2018, Luna focused in part on the creative ways queer migrants negotiate relationships despite geopolitical borders. For example, she described how technology helped her navigate a new relationship across borders (Manalansan 2005; Francisco-Menchavez 2018). Luna made it a point to tell me that she is in love again and, after fourteen years of living in LA, plans to return to Mexico to live with the woman she loves. "I know her from the pueblo. She's married and has her kids. We've been long distance for four years now and will be together when I go back." While chatrooms have long been a way for queer migrant women to connect with other women, new technology platforms allow for more personalized connections, the ability to spend time together (virtually), and make plans for a life together. The two women have nurtured their relationship digitally, using technology like Facebook and WhatsApp, a messaging application that allows for text and video communication, and the sharing of photos. Despite her family not supporting her decision, she feels that she has to give herself a chance to be happy again. Given the trauma of her last border-crossing experience and the fear of not being able to return to the United States if she left, she hadn't risked returning to Mexico, even when close family members died. However, after all this time spent living in fear, she decided that giving herself a chance to be happy again was worth the risk. Soon after our interview, I learned through her Facebook posts that she has indeed made her way back to Mexico. Luna did not allow the physical border between them, and the potential impossibility of returning to the United States, to impede her from following her path towards love and physical proximity with her new partner. Technology has had a more bitter function for Dulce, however, who reports that her mother keeps in touch with all of her siblings via Facebook but has deleted her as a friend. Where technology created opportunities for Luna to create and nurture love and kinship, Dulce's mother has harnessed technology to foreclose even a digital relationship.

Crossing borders

Migration across borders is intimately tied to familial networks and kinship. For Luna, helping, being with, and seeking family were among the reasons for her multiple migrations. When discussing why she considers her former partner Lety part of her family, Luna explains: "I think that because of the horrible experience we shared crossing the border, that united us. We're just friends now." The experience she refers to was Luna's last journey across the border from Mexico to the U.S. in 2004, one that almost cost her and Lety their lives. After getting lost from the *coyote* [smuggler] and the rest of the group with which they crossed, they spent days walking through the Arizona desert until reaching Santa Rosa, a town almost 100 miles from Tucson. On the way, they ran out of food and water. "Lety's feet were so swollen that she almost wanted to give up and stay there, but I wouldn't allow it. I encouraged her to continue," Luna recalls. She talked about having to drink dirty water from a trough where animals fed at a ranch they found along the way, and about a Native family offering them food. When night fell, in a spot away from the main ranch house, they made a bed out of leaves and hay and, in the middle of the night, they awoke to a pack of barking dogs hovering over them. "The dogs finally went away close to dawn. It was terrifying."

Luna's migration narrative began long before this experience, in the 1980s when she crossed multiple borders to be with her first lover, Chole, a childhood friend who used to work with her in the fields in Guanajuato. Throughout our interview, she mapped the back-and-forth trajectory of her life as a migrant worker, beginning in Guanajuato, Mexico, travelling to the U.S.-Mexico border, to Arizona and Texas, back to Mexico, and finally to LA, her narratives summarizing twenty years of crossing the borderlands back and forth as a migrant farm worker. She mapped out her childhood in Mexico, discussing how her father's absence affected her and how she started working at a young age to help her mother with expenses. She talked about having to marry a man and birthing a child at a young age due to societal expectations, and about the pain of sending her daughter to the U.S. so she could have a better life with her father. She told me of falling in love for the first time at age fifteen while working in the fields: "The girl's name was Chole and it was a secret relationship, supposedly, even though everyone knew we were everywhere together.... It was 1985, close to the time of Amnesty in the U.S. We would easily cross back and forth," she says, situating herself historically and politically within the U.S. immigration narrative and referring to times when restrictions at the U.S.-Mexico border were not as strict.[3] Luna and Chole had been thinking of leaving their small town and, in order to be together, they came north to a small village in Baja California near the Arizona border. Working seasonally in cotton fields, she recalled, "I'm not ashamed but it is true. We cried from the cold because we slept under trees."

Luna and Chole's trips together to the border were not only about finding the freedom to be together, but also making a living as itinerant workers who helped their families. They worked, made money, and enjoyed being together for three to four months at a time. Eventually, tired of moving back and forth and seeking more stability, they decided to cross into the United States. "We were living in el Ejido Cuervos near San Luis Río Colorado, working in cotton, cleaning watermelon, cantaloupe, in whatever it was until infidelity came into our lives," Luna related, referring to how Chole cheated on her. Her memories of crossing with Chole are different than her last traumatic experience with Lety. Overall, Luna's mapping of desire and love cannot be disconnected from issues of class, migration, labor, and sexuality, affirming the late sociologist Lionel Cantú's notion of a "queer political economy" that centers sexuality as a contributing reason people migrate (2009).

Since the 1980s, many Guatemalan migrants, have fled to the U.S.—and LA—seeking political asylum (Hamilton and Chinchilla Stoltz 2001), but not all Guatemalan women in Los Angeles migrated of their own volition (Kopahl 1998). For example, in Gabrielle Kopahl's study on Guatemalan women in LA, the decision for the women to migrate was made by their mothers. This was also the case for Dulce, who cites two different reasons why her mother arranged her migration: Dulce's teenage conflicts with her mother and the potential escalation of violence when two jealous boyfriends began fighting over her. Thus, ongoing and potential domestic violence played a pivotal role in Dulce leaving her country. For Dulce, despite the traumatic circumstances, leaving Guatemala meant freedom from her mother's physical abuse and the patriarchal dictates of the church pastor. Her story is an example of how many Guatemalan women's migration narratives are bound to toxic masculinist violence. In addition, Dulce's initial experience crossing the border was impacted by intersecting class, gender, and racial factors:

> My mom sent me and told the coyote, who was a woman, "My daughter is a virgin." The coyote's boyfriend heard it and the woman was protecting me all of the time. She kept saying, "Don't look at my boyfriend." I was with a friend who was blonde and green-eyed, so she was treated well in Mexico. We stayed two weeks in el DF [Mexico City], and [it] took us two months to get there.... When we got to Mexico City, a policeman knew that I was a migrant and he told me, "You don't have to go. You can come to live [with] me." He tried to convince me. Other girls who were afraid may have stayed; you know?... It was a good experience. My uncle picked me up when I arrived [in the U.S.], but after I left [the safe house], Immigration came to the house about thirty minutes after. I was very lucky.

Dulce's comments about her journey from Guatemala to the United States are unlike those of many fellow migrants, who report having terrible experiences. She recognizes that her age and virginity were factors in the female *coyote's* protectiveness towards her, and while her journey could have been precarious, traveling with a White-passing friend through Mexico provided a safety net, as was being light-skinned and femme-presenting herself. She also recognizes how fortunate timing and the presence of a male family member to escort her from the safe house not long after she arrived saved her from being detained by U.S. immigration officials.

Leisure Spaces: Plaza

Bars and clubs have been important sites of belonging for queer migrants in Los Angeles, including Luna and Dulce. As Elizabeth Lapovsky Kennedy and Madeline Davis (1993) have demonstrated, bars were significant sites of belonging for working lesbian women in 1940s Buffalo, New York. Similarly, in LA, bars such as Redz in Boyle Heights have been a site of sexual discovery.[4] Although not as prominent as those that cater to gay men, social spaces for lesbians and queer women are still significant for community formation, especially for working-class and gender nonconforming women (Faderman and Timmons 2009). However, as in other cities, such spaces are disappearing in LA at faster rates than establishments that cater to gay men. When I asked Luna and Dulce about social or leisure spaces in LA that were significant to them as Latina lesbian migrants, they each invoked the Plaza nightclub on Santa Monica Boulevard and La Brea. Plaza has catered to Latinx patrons for over twenty years, with a drag show catering mostly to queer, sexual and gender non-conforming women (Steelman 2015). As such, Plaza renders visible the existence of lesbian migrants in the city and is not only an important memory site for many queer Latinx Angelenos, both immigrants and U.S.-born, but continues to foster affirmation and community among them.

Traditionally, respectable Latina women are not supposed to frequent bars without a man, so for both narrators, Plaza represented a site of contestation and liberation. However, as queer women, leisure spaces such as bars are not only places to experience community, find friends and lovers, but also sites of experimentation, venues for traversing sexual, gendered, and migratory boundaries. Going out to these bars, then, is a form of "leisure as political practice" (Shaw 2001, 186) and of finding sequins in the rubble. Many queer Latinxs in LA first figured out their queer identities in clubs. In a rapidly gentrifying LA where queer working-class spaces are disappearing, mapping queer migrant geographies is important for preserving city memory. Plaza is part of a queer immigrant "people's guide to Los Angeles" (Pulido, Barraclough, and Cheng, 2012). Although Luna recalls that the first bar she went to in LA was Silverlake Lounge, which also caters to Latinx immigrant patrons, Plaza was where she remembers having the most fun and feeling most among a community:

> I liked it because there are lots of women there and because of the [drag] show. The first time I went was with a woman, Egri, whom I knew from my hometown. She was married when she came here but then came out. I knew that she had turned lesbian. I was in Mexico [at the time], so when I arrived, I asked my daughter, "Can you get me her number?" and she did. She took me to Plaza and it was a party every week either at Plaza or at her house. Although I was still technically with Lety, our relationship was ending and one day we had been drinking and I told Egri, "Can I tell you something? Would you like to be my *amante* [lover]? She said yes [laughter].

For Luna, going out to Plaza allowed her to have fun while negotiating the trauma she had just experienced a few months prior while crossing the border with Lety. Plaza was also where she developed a connection with another queer migrant (Egri, her new lover), who she already knew from her hometown. Egri's home and, to some degree, Plaza functioned as what Lionel Cantú (2009) calls a "landing pad" where immigrant gay men (and, in Luna's case, lesbian women) can begin creating their lives in the city as newcomers.

For her part, Dulce enthusiastically remembered that the first time she went to Plaza was with her then-husband, who often went to the bar after work with friends but had never before taken her along. She remembers that, when she got there, she looked around, saw lesbians and drag queens, and had that "aha" moment. "This is what I am. It was shocking for me. I felt like 'Oh my God! This is me!' I finally could put a name to what I was." She made a connection to the first time she felt an attraction for a woman back in Guatemala: "I was at a funeral for a neighbor and there was a beautiful Black woman there. My mom told me to go offer her a *tamal*. Everyone knew she was a *marimacho*, that's what we called lesbians there. I didn't know that word [lesbian] until I got here. When I went up to her and gave her the food, I felt something for her."

Dulce's experience at Plaza gave her a newfound understanding of her initial feelings of attraction for a woman, which she had initially dismissed in part because of the pejorative term *marimacho*. In Los Angeles and at this club, Dulce was able to embrace her sexual desires and identity as a lesbian. In her personal cartography of LA, Plaza is meaningful because it was the place where she first had the realization that she was a lesbian after struggling with her feelings for so many years. Both of these memories—her first time at Plaza and the beautiful woman at the funeral in her hometown—were pivotal moments in her long journey towards her sexual identity. After she discovered Plaza (and in short order came out and left her husband), she started partying a lot: "[For] years after [first] going to Plaza I've enjoyed going out. Arena, Circus, Executive Suite, Pride. I don't go out as much anymore but oh my God I used to love it." The place of nightlife in her memories is important to her journey on a personal level and for the social significance it carries.

Scholars like Yessica García Hernandez (2016) highlight the importance of self-determined leisure and pleasure for Latinas. Like the women Hernandez writes about, Luna and Dulce exhibit "a love and pleasure for oneself that is not typically sanctioned for women in Latina immigrant spaces," including for Latina lesbian immigrants. García Hernandez argues that Latinas must navigate respectability politics as they prioritize their own pleasure and "traverse both the politics of home and the nightclub" and that "*parrandiando*" [partying] is a "radical act that shamelessly seeks pleasures without being concerned about depending on or satisfying men" (2016). For Dulce and Luna, then, Plaza became not only a site of knowledge production of self through exploration of their sexual and gendered identities, but also functioned as a reprieve from the normativities and restrictions of everyday immigrant life. As a place where they could socialize with fellow immigrants, *buchas* [butches], trans women, and drag performers, Plaza was a space of queer migrant worldmaking and a stop on their journey toward themselves.

Conclusion

Dulce and Luna's multiple journeys feature migrations across geopolitical borders to the United States and back and an exploration of their desires, values, gendered identities; journeys towards their personal sexual freedom and self-autonomy despite multiple obstacles. Gloria Anzaldúa's philosophies shed light on the multiple selves and journeys that become what she calls "the path of *conocimiento*" or the path towards consciousness (Anzaldúa and Keating 2002). On both sides of the physical border, Dulce and Luna have had to negotiate family relationships, redefine themselves, and seek freedom. As they shared their journeys with me, both were very self-reflective, emphasizing moments that shaped them. Among its multiple meanings, then, finding sequins in the rubble is about this journey across borders and into multiple selves, a path toward what Anzaldúa refers to as "mestiza consciousness" or "*la facultad*," the ability of *mestizas* or mixed-race women to navigate the oppressive structures they inhabit, as well as the historical legacy they have inherited, while reinterpreting history, redefining themselves, and developing a "tolerance for contradiction and ambiguity" (Anzaldúa 1987, 100, 101). After Dulce and Luna embarked on their journeys from their respective countries to the U.S., they had to navigate LA as racialized, working poor migrants, even as they uncovered and navigated more fulfilling and introspective gendered and sexual selves aided by their erotic encounters and connections with other women. Their realizations of having traversed many paths to their selfhoods, which came through in the interviews through reflection, truth telling, and recognition of fragmentation, mirror Anzaldúa's path of *conocimiento*. As Anzaldúa suggests, this knowledge comes from "accepting your own authority to direct rather than letting others run you" (1987, 571). Through self-reflection, each narrator has arrived at a place of awareness of her own agency, recognizing that she is a work in progress and that her choices are now guided by the desire to find love and continue to grow. This process is not one of a neoliberal subject moving towards "progress," but rather about how the quotidian functions as revolutionary; there is no end point, no "arrival," only the iterative process of shifting, discerning, and adjusting.

While here I focus predominantly on advantages associated with Dulce and Luna's lives in LA, this does not mean that the United States is necessarily physically safer for them than their places of origin, given the institutionalized intersections of misogyny, homophobia, and violence toward perceived immigrants now rampant in the U.S. For queer migrants, safety is both complicated and relative. Latina lesbians find fortitude in "their struggle by transforming their obstacles into a new consciousness" (Acosta 2008, 655). So, rather than a consequence of being in the United States *per se*, the safety Dulce and Luna each experienced was due to the knowledge and power gained from their respective physical, mental, and emotional journeys.

This oral history project builds on prior feminist Latina, Chicana, queer of color and lesbian oral history projects (Ruiz 2008; Wat 2001; Roque Ramírez 2006; Creel Falcón 2018). Dulce and Luna are not self-proclaimed feminists, but they *are*, like the authors in *This Bridge Called My Back*, enacting liberatory praxis in their everyday lives and by theorizing and telling their stories. Without wishing to appropriate Luna and Dulce's words, speak for them or distort their stories, but conscious of the shared construction of knowledge in the oral history process, I have underscored the value of their words and what we can learn from them in historical, political, or personal and intimate ways. I've mapped some aspects of their personal transformations—how they were taken apart, but even more, how they put themselves back together—through their own everyday practices and intimacies. The stories presented here show everyday acts of resilience as revolutionary, not because they are breaking down institutions *per se*, but because, as woman of color feminists have argued for a long time, everyday acts in the face of a world that denies one's existence are revolutionary in and of themselves. Perhaps, through unearthing more stories like theirs, queer migrants become legible within mainstream narratives of migrants and queer communities. Their journeys have much to teach us about the intersections of migration, space, love, desire, and kinship, and speak to what queer migration scholars argue about the intersections between borders, migration, political economy, sexuality, and gender. These are day-to-day acts of everyday women, *lesbianas* who are actively creating their journey, making choices towards freedom—economic, social, and erotic freedom—in their process of finding sequins in the rubble.

Notes

1. On the importance and politics of the archive archive, see Taylor (2003).
2. Brackets indicate clarification by author.
3. Amnesty is shorthand for Immigration Reform and Control Act, which was signed and passed into law in 1986. http://library.uwb.edu/Static/USimmigration/1986_immigration_reform_and_control_act.html
4. Redz, which closed in 2015, was formerly known as Redheads and Reds.

References

Abrego, Leisy. 2014. *Sacrificing Families: Navigating Laws, Labor and Love across Borders*. Palo Alto, CA: Stanford University Press.

Acosta, Katie L. 2008. "Lesbianas in the Borderlands: Shifting Identities and Imagined Communities." *Gender and Society* 22(5): 639–655.

Alamilla Boyd, Nan and Horacio Roque Ramírez. 2009. *Bodies of Evidence: The Practice of Queer Oral History*. Oxford, England: Oxford University Press.

Alvarez Jr., Eddy Francisco. 2016. "Finding Sequins in the Rubble: Stitching Together and Archive of Trans Latina Los Angeles." *TSQ: Transgender Studies Quarterly* 3(4): 618–627.

Anzaldúa, Gloria. 1987. *Borderlands/La Frontera: The New Mestiza*. Berkeley, CA: Aunt Lute Press.

Anzaldúa, Gloria E. and Ana Louise Keating. 2002. *This Bridge We Call Home: Radical Visions for Transformation*. New York, NY: Routledge.

Borges, Sandibel. 2015. "Not Coming Out, but Building Home: An Oral History in Reconceptualizing a Queer Migrant Home." *Diálogo* 18(2): 119–130.

Cantú Jr., Lionel. 2009. *The Sexuality of Migration: Border Crossings and Mexican Immigrant Men*, edited by Nancy Naples and Salvador Vidal Ortiz. New York, NY: New York University Press.

Cárdenas, Maritza E. 2018. *Constituting Central American-Americans: Transnational Identities and the Politics of Dislocation*. New Brunswick, NJ: Rutgers University Press.

Chavez, Karma. 2013. *Queer Migration Politics: Activist Rhetoric and Coalitional Possibilities*. Chicago, IL: University of Illinois Press.

Chinchilla, Maya and Karina Alvarado. 2009. *Desde el Epicentro: An Anthology of US Central American Poetry and Art*. Los Angeles, CA: Chapbook.

Creel Falcón, Kandace. 2018. "Friday Night Tacos: Exploring Midwestern Borderlands through Familia Women's Oral Histories." *Chicana/Latina Studies* 17(1): 66–93.

Crenshaw, Kimberlé. 1992. "Whose Story is it Anyway? Feminist and Antiracist Appropriations of Anita Hill." In *Race-Ing, En-Gendering Power: Essays on Anita Hill, Clarence Thomas, and the Construction of Social Reality*, edited by Toni Morrison, 402-436. New York, NY: Pantheon Books.

Faderman, Lillian and Stuart Timmons. 2009. *Gay L.A.: A History of Sexual Outlaws, Power Politics, and Lipstick Lesbians*. Berkeley, CA: University of California Press.

Francisco-Menchavez, Valerie. 2018. *The Labor of Care: Filipina Migrants and Transnational Families in the Digital Age*. Urbana, IL: University of Illinois Press.

García Hernandez, Yessica. 2016. "Intoxication as Feminist Pleasure: Drinking, Dancing, and Un-Dressing with/for Jenni Rivera." *NANO* Issue 9, https://nanocrit.com/issues/issue9/intoxication-feminist-pleasure-drinking-dancing-and-un-dressing-jenni-rivera

González-López, Gloria. 2005. *Erotic Journeys: Mexican Immigrants and their Sex Lives*. Berkeley, CA: University of California Press.

Goodman, Leo A. 1961. "Snowball Sampling." *The Annals of Mathematical Statistics* 32(1): 148–170.

Hamilton, Nora and Norma Chinchilla Stoltz. 2001. *Seeking Community in a Global City: Guatemalans and Salvadorans in Los Angeles*. Philadelphia, PA: Temple University Press.

Kopahl, Gabrielle. 1998. *Voices of Guatemalan Women in Los Angeles: Understanding their Immigration*. New York, NY: Garland Publishing, Inc.

Lapovsky Kennedy, Elizabeth and Madeline D. Davis. 1993. *Boots of Leather, Slippers of Gold: The History of a Lesbian Community*. New York, NY: Routledge.

Luibhéid, Eithne. 2002. *Entry Denied: Controlling Sexuality at the Border*. Minneapolis, MN: University of Minnesota Press.

Manalansan IV, Martin. 2005. "Migrancy, Modernity, Mobility: Quotidian Struggles and Queer Diasporic Intimacy." In *Queer Migrations: Sexuality, U.S. Citizenship and Border Crossings*, edited by Eithne Luibhéid and Lionel Cantú Jr., 146–160. Minneapolis, MN: University of Minnesota Press.

Menjívar, Cecilia. 2011. *Enduring Violence: Ladina Women's Lives in Guatemala*. Berkeley, CA: University of California Press.

Mills, Robert. 2006. "Queer is Here? Lesbian, Gay, Bisexual and Transgender Histories and Public Culture." *History Workshop Journal* 62: 253–263.

Moraga, Cherríe. 2015. "La Güera." In *This Bridge Called My Back: Writings by Radical Women of Color*, edited by Cherríe Moraga and Gloria Anzaldúa, 22–29. Albany, NY: SUNY Press.

Muñoz, José Esteban. 1999. *Disidentifications: Queers of Color and the Performance of Politics*. Minneapolis, MN: University of Minnesota Press.

Portillo, Suyapa. 2012. "The Los Angeles May Day 'Queer Contingent' and the Politics of Inclusion," *Huffington Post*, May 5, 2012, http://www.huffingtonpost.com/suyapa-portillo/the-los-angeles-may-day-q_b_1476762.html

Pulido, Laura, Laura Barraclough, and Wendy Cheng. 2012. *A People's Guide to Los Angeles*. Berkeley, CA: University of California Press.

Raleigh Yow, Valerie. 2005. *Recording Oral History: A Guide for the Humanities and Social Sciences*. Lanham, MD: Altamira Press.

Ramírez, Marla Andrea. 2018. "The Making of Mexican Illegality: Immigration Exclusions Based on Race, Class Status, and Gender." *New Political Science* 40(2): 317–335.

Rodríguez, Juana María. 2003. *Queer Latinidad: Identity Practices and Discursive Spaces*. New York, NY: NYU Press.

Roque Ramírez, Horacio N. 2006. "A Living Archive of Desire: Teresita La Campesina and the Embodiment of Queer Latino Community Histories." In *Archive Stories: Facts, Fiction, and the Writing of History*, edited by Antoinette Burton, 111–135. Durham, NC: Duke University Press.

Ruiz, Vicki. 2008. *From Out of the Shadows: Mexican Women in Twentieth-Century America*. Oxford, England: Oxford University Press.

Saavedra, Cinthya M. and Ellen D. Nymark. 2014. "Borderland-Mestizaje Feminism: The New Tribalism." In *Handbook of Critical and Indigenous Methodologies*, edited by Norman K. Denzin, Yvonne S. Lincoln, and Linda Tuhiwai Smith, 255–276. Los Angeles, CA: Sage.

Sandoval, Chela. 1997. "Mestizaje as Method: Feminists of Color Challenge the Canon." In *Living Chicana Theory*, edited by Carla Trujillo, 353–370. San Francisco, CA: Third Woman Press.

Shaw, Susan M. 2001. "Conceptualizing Resistance: Women's Leisure as Political Practice."*Journal of Leisure Research* 33(2): 186–201.

Steelman, Katherine. 2015. "Home(bodies): Transitory Belonging at LA's Oldest Latina/o Drag Bar." Presentation at "Latina/o Utopias: Future Forms and the Will of Literature," April 24, 2015.

Taylor, Diana. 2003. *The Archive and the Repertoire: Performing Cultural Memory in the Americas*. Durham, NC: Duke University Press.

Torres, Lourdes. 2018. "Latinx?" *Latino Studies* 16(3): 283–285.

Wat, Eric. 2001. *The Making of a Gay Asian Community: An Oral History of Pre-AIDS Los Angeles*. Lanham, MD: Rowman and Littlefield.

"We have to do *a lot* of healing": LGBTQ migrant Latinas resisting and healing from systemic violence

Sandibel Borges

ABSTRACT
Using narratives from oral histories of LGBTQ migrant Latinas in Los Angeles, California, and Mexico City, Mexico, this article argues that, despite experiences of oppression, the narrators practice resistance in their daily lives. The article first addresses how the narrators confront conditions of detainability and deportability, making survival a constant struggle. It then presents different ways in which the narrators engage in resistance, from survival to community building and activism. Finally, it argues that healing is a key factor in the narrators' resistance—healing functions as both a tool for and outcome of resistance.

Migration to the United States occurs for many reasons, including economic necessity, family reunification, fleeing domestic and/or political violence, or a combination.[1] Yet U.S. anti-immigration discourses and anti-LGBTQ rhetoric and policy deeply impact the lives of LGBTQ migrant Latinas. Indeed, anti-immigration rhetoric never functions alone, but is intermeshed with heteronormativity, white supremacy, and exploitation resulting in the surveillance and disposability of queer migrants (Luibhéid 2002, 2005; Pérez 2003; Chávez 2011). In this article, I present the narratives of five LGBTQ migrant Latinas based on oral histories. My framework builds on insights from women of color feminisms, queer of color critique, and queer migration studies to explore the relationship between the intersecting oppressions that LGBTQ migrant Latinas experience and the resistance they practice, the latter being key in their healing processes. I argue that the narrators engage in different forms of resistance, making their queer migrant lives livable under conditions of violence (Muñoz 2009; Chávez 2013). Their resistance is especially urgent given the ongoing policing of their bodies, quite literally making their survival a constant struggle.

The narrators practice resistance through daily survival, building communities, and engaging in activism with other LGBTQ migrants of color. I further propose that practices of resistance are necessary for the narrators' healing and, in turn, healing functions as a tool for continuous resistance.

Practicing resistance and healing in a community contradicts the isolation, displacement, and social abandonment created by systems of migration, heteronormativity, and white supremacy.

The five narrators are Claudia, Imelda, Anabel, Susana, and Yanelia. When signing the consent forms, some narrators chose pseudonyms, while others requested that I use their real names. I conducted the interviews between 2013 and 2015 in Los Angeles, California, and Mexico City, Mexico. Narrators were all in their mid- to late twenties. Claudia, Imelda, and Anabel lived in Los Angeles while Yanelia and Susana lived in Mexico City after having spent much of their lives in the United States. Anabel was born in Peru, migrated to Chile at the age of four and to the United States at thirteen with her family. She returned with her family to Chile after one year and migrated alone back to the U.S. at eighteen. The other four narrators are from Mexico and migrated to the United States between the ages of three and six. At the time of the interviews, Imelda and Claudia were undocumented. Claudia used the terms "queer" and "lesbian," while Imelda used "queer," "two-spirit," and "fluid" to define their sexualities. Yanelia and Susana were trying to regularize their immigration status to return to the United States; both used the identities "gay" and "lesbian" to define their sexualities. Anabel was in the process of applying for a green card to become a U.S. permanent resident and identified as "queer" and "gay-queer." They all defined their gender as women. Except for Susana, the narrators had all completed a college education in the United States. The five narrators defined their class status as poor and working-class. Finally, Imelda, Claudia, and Anabel did community work in their everyday lives, including but not limited to community organizing. Claudia and Imelda used the term *undocuqueer* to define their activism.

The narrators told their stories from positions of vulnerability. As individuals whose movements are constantly under surveillance, some narrators chose not to share certain experiences and, in some cases, they told their stories to challenge the silences about queer migrant lives. This article honors the narrators' voices, silences, and reasons for telling/not telling parts of their stories.

Note on terminology

Throughout this article I use the terms *migrant*, *LGBTQ*, and *queer*. Borrowing from Eithne Luibhéid (2005, xi), I understand and use "migrant" as "anyone who has crossed an international border to reach the United States," or any other country, without making a "distinction among legal immigrants, refugees, asylum seekers, and undocumented immigrants." These different "categories" of migrants, she argues, are created and defined by the state, which then determine the types of rights, or lack thereof, which individuals in each are permitted to claim. Similarly, Patricia Zavella (2011, xiii) uses the term "migrant" "to evoke the ambiguities and indeterminacies that are involved in the process of migration as well as to focus on those who are residing within the United States but who may also engage in transnational relations." These ambiguities in migration processes are precisely encompassed in the categories that Luibhéid lays out earlier, which shift depending on the circumstances. Like Zavella, I address experiences of people who "engage in transnational relations" between the United States and Mexico, applicable to migrants who live in the United States as well as those who have returned to Mexico. My use of the term "migrant" thus speaks to the complexities of migration systems and of individuals who are caught in them.

I use the acronym LGBTQ to loosely categorize the narrators as individuals who do not embody or embrace heteronormative genders or sexualities. I use it with caution, remaining aware that these categories are not transhistorical (Somerville 1994; Luibhéid 2008). That is, the terms in the acronym have only been used in contemporary history and have not remained fixed. They are not transnational, either. The categories have been largely applied within Western contexts and reproduced by Western, colonial, and imperial processes that overshadow terminologies utilized by Indigenous peoples and other racialized populations in the global North and South (Luibhéid 2005; Driskill et al. 2011; MacDonald 2010). The limitations of the acronym are revealed by how narrators, as described earlier, define their genders as women and their sexualities as gay, lesbian, queer, fluid, and gay-queer. They do not neatly fit LGBTQ, nor do I claim that they do. LGBTQ also runs the risk of flattening difference. While it is an acronym that requires questioning, in this article it serves the strategic purpose of loosely referring to individuals who have been systematically defined as deviant by the U.S. nation-state.

Similarly, I use queer as a term that is intended to respect narrators' self-identification, not in a universalizing way. Importantly, scholars have largely critiqued the use of "queer" as an identity label (Haritaworn and Kuntsman 2014; Butler 1999). For example, Judith Butler suggests that "the mobilization of identity categories for the purposes of politicization always remain threatened by the prospect of identity becoming an instrument of the power one opposes" (Butler 1999, xxvii). From this perspective, queer-as-identity might reproduce essentialist notions of gender and sexuality, which the term "queer" precisely intends to destabilize. However, given that narrators used it to position themselves, I am in agreement with José Esteban Muñoz (1999, 5) when he argues that "any narrative of identity that reduces subjectivity to either a social constructivist model or what has been called an essentialist understanding of the self is especially exhausted." Such is the case because "neither story is complete" (5). When I use "queer" as the narrators' own self-identification, it is neither to essentialize identity—to claim that identity is fixed, inherent, and that it defines their entire existence—nor to claim that it is merely socially constructed and therefore not real. Instead, I refer to "queer" as a social location that some narrators embraced as part of a process that defined their non-heterosexuality at the time of the interviews.

I also use the term "queer" as an "oppositional critique of heteronormativity and an interest in the ambiguity of gender and sexuality" (Driskill et al. 2011, 3). Using queer as an oppositional critique allows me to approach it, like Karma R. Chávez (2013) and José Muñoz (2009) conceptualize it, as that which makes lives livable. Therefore, when I say "queer migrations," I am referring to migrations that are oppositional, messy, and that bring into question the normalization of migration systems as these intersect with hetero- and homonormativity. Actively challenging systems of power creates possibilities for making oppressed lives livable. It is this messiness and oppositional-ness that has the potential to open up spaces of resistance against the very systems that keep LGBTQ Latina migrants marginalized.

Methodology

I gathered the data in this article during the completion of my doctoral dissertation on LGBTQ migrations and resistance in the field of feminist studies. I conducted fieldwork in Los Angeles, California, from 2013 to 2014, and in Mexico City, Mexico, from 2014 to 2016 (data in this article are from 2013 to 2015). To recruit narrators, I created flyers in English and Spanish asking for the participation of LGBT, queer, or non-heterosexual Latina migrants in a research project on LGBTQ migration. It invited people of all ethnicities and heritages who were eighteen or older to participate. The flyers included my direct contact information. I sent the flyers to individuals and organizations, asking them to circulate them among their contacts, and followed up by using the snowball method. Interviews lasted between one and a half to three hours.

My positionality is relevant to the rapport I built with the narrators and to the ways they told their stories. I am a self-identified queer migrant Mexicana[2]; I was raised poor and working-class and became an immigrant in the United States at the age of thirteen. I am bilingual; I speak Spanish and English, with English being my second language. Finally, I was between the ages of twenty-seven and thirty when I completed my fieldwork. Researching LGBTQ migration gave me the opportunity to hear other queer migration stories and at times share my own. However, coming from academia, one of my goals was to remain intentional about not reproducing exploitative research practices. As I explained my research approach to one narrator in Los Angeles, she looked me in the eye and said, "*mujer* [woman], you are one of us." There was a sense of trust with the narrators, and we often switched between English, Spanish, and Spanglish during and outside interviews. Nevertheless, I remain aware that power dynamics are always present and that some narrators did not tell parts of their stories precisely because of my position in academia and the role academic research has played in extracting knowledge from marginalized communities. My hope is to bring to the forefront the narratives that the interviewees shared, which are representative of their resistance and healing. In honoring their preferred language, in this article I offer the original quotes followed by English translation when necessary.

Policing queer migrant bodies: LGBTQ migrant Latinas struggling to survive

The U.S. immigration system polices the narrators' bodies, resulting in survival being a constant struggle. Importing and deporting migrants has formed a major part of the United States imperial history and its formation as a nation-state, even while presenting the immigration system as one for which migrants should be grateful. In the contemporary context, migrants are racially profiled on a regular basis, regardless of their legal status (Romero 2006; Fischer 2013). Given the collaboration between local and state police, and Immigration and Customs Enforcement (ICE), this profiling often results in the deportation of undocumented migrants (Fischer 2013). Indeed, the Department of Homeland Security recorded 385,100 deportations in FY2010, increasing to 391,953 in FY2011 (Simanski and Sapp 2012, 4). The numbers of detentions in ICE facilities also increased from 363,064 in FY2010 to 429,247 in FY2011 (5). Countries of origin with the highest percentages of detentions were Mexico, Guatemala, Honduras, and El Salvador. LGBTQ migrants are among the detained and deported; the Williams Institute estimate that approximately 267,000 undocumented individuals living in the United States identified as LGBT (Gates 2013, 1).[3] This number is likely to be an undercount as migrants, especially older adults, are often reluctant to identify as such (2). Yet it is clear that LGBTQ migrants confront conditions of being undocumented, detainable, and deportable.

Susana's narrative exemplifies surviving migrant detention and deportation as a lesbian woman of color. She first migrated as a small child in 1994 from Mexico to California, then to Kansas, and finally settled in Oklahoma as her working-class family searched for better economic opportunities. At the time of our interview, Susana identified as *lesbian*—in English. She said the Spanish word *"lesbiana"* felt harsh, like an insult. Her gender presentation could be labeled as masculine of center, with Susana describing herself as *"una mujer más masculina"* (a more masculine woman). After living in Oklahoma for many years, Susana was detained in 2010 for a traffic violation. She thought the violation would result in going to court and paying a fine, but instead she was taken to the David Larry Moss Criminal Justice Center in Tulsa, Oklahoma, where she spent six months awaiting a court date. Susana was originally placed in detention for one year, but was released early and required to wait for a hearing in her home in Oklahoma. In court, she advocated for herself, as the immigration lawyer she hired did and said nothing to help her. Susana was given the "choice" between deportation and voluntary departure; she picked voluntary departure.

The U.S. Citizenship and Immigration Services (n.d.) defines voluntary departure as granting migrants "the privilege" of leaving the United States without a removal order, thereby "avoid[ing] the adverse future consequences under the immigration laws attributable to having been removed." One of the adverse consequences of removal is being barred from ever entering the country legally again (Simanski and Sapp 2012, 2). Framing this particular type of deportation as "voluntary," a "privilege," and a "choice" masks how the immigration system disposes of migrants. Meanwhile, it constructs the immigration system as benevolent, working for migrants' interests, for which migrants should be grateful. In reality, the immigration system is invested in migrants' dehumanization and criminalization (Chang 2016).

When I asked Susana about her experiences as a woman and a lesbian in detention, where guards were both female and male, Susana said she never felt harassed or intimidated by anyone. She was reluctant to speak about her specific experiences as lesbian in or outside detention, insisting that her sexuality was not a factor in her treatment by guards or other detainees. Referring to her lesbian identity, Susana stated:

> *No siento que haya que esconderlo pero tampoco siento que sea algo súper importante. No es como que diga, "¡soy lesbiana, celébrenme!" Sí es parte de mi, no lo escondo, pero no es algo que me haga más ni menos.* (I don't feel like it should be hidden, but I don't think it's something super important, either. I'm not like, "I'm a lesbian, celebrate me!" It is part of who I am, I don't hide it, but it's not something that makes me any more or less).

Susana did remember some of the other women in detention showing curiosity about her sexuality:

> *Siempre me preguntaban [si era lesbian] [laughs]. Bueno, más que preguntar they knew, se puede decir.* They were like, oh okay, you're like that, okay. *Y así. No era en*

plan de molestarme; nunca me he sentido hostigada por eso. (They would always ask me [if I was lesbian] [laughs]. More than asking, you could say that they knew. They were like, oh okay, you're like that, okay; things like that. It was never with the intention to bother me. I've never felt harassed for that).

Nevertheless, during a different part of our conversation, Susana expressed that harassment: "*es normal para mi, ya no me molesta*" (is normal for me, it no longer bothers me). Perceiving harassment as normal seems to be part of Susana's refusal to perceive and present herself as a victim, her way of fighting feeling powerless. Her refusal could also derive from the pressure to feel grateful and not complain because she had the "privilege" of receiving voluntary departure instead of removal and she did not experience great harm in or outside detention for being lesbian. It is also possible that Susana intentionally avoids giving any attention to homophobic violence as a survival tactic to lessen the pain it produces, especially as she tries to simultaneously navigate having been policed and detained as an undocumented migrant of color who was ultimately deported.

Similar to Susana, Yanelia's narrative demonstrates conditions facing LGBTQ migrants who are detained and deported. To Yanelia, however, it was important to name her lesbian identity as a defining factor in her journey, along with being a migrant and working-poor. At the time of our interview, Yanelia identified as lesbian and was femme presenting. Yanelia migrated three times to the United States: at the ages of six, eight, and ten with her parents. When she was sixteen, her father, a lawful permanent resident, petitioned to legalize her immigration status. Seven years later, she received a letter from the immigration services giving her an appointment in Ciudad Juárez, Chihuaha, Mexico. She planned to attend, thinking that she would return to the United States shortly thereafter. But because as a child she had entered the country three times without authorization, she was punished and banned from re-entering the country for ten years.

During her interview at the consulate in Ciudad Juárez, which Yanelia attended with a female friend, she was asked questions that went beyond her immigration status.

> I have a tattoo that I got... it says "friendship." It's in Chinese... I had just turned twenty-one and I was like, "sure I'll get it," you know? But they thought it was like a gang sign or something. That was another thing that did not play in my favor.

Yanelia believes that being a Mexican undocumented migrant with a tattoo became synonymous with being seen as a gang member and criminal. She was further questioned about her sexuality:

> They [immigration officials] also kind of asked awkward questions, like, "Are you sure she's your friend?" I'm like, "Yes, I'm telling you she's my friend." Supposedly, they check your Facebook, you know? I've always been open about my sexuality; I'm not going to deny that I'm gay.[4]

Although the exclusion of gay and lesbian migration was formally removed from U.S. immigration law in 1990 (Luibhéid 2002, 2005; Naples and Vidal-Ortiz 2009), Yanelia's experience reveals the heteronormative and white supremacist nature of the immigration system. In the early 1900s, U.S. borders were reinforced to keep so-called sexual deviants and non-whites out, only opening for cheap labor and increasingly criminalizing those who did not belong in the white heteronormative nation (Luibhéid 2005, xiv; Pérez 2003). Indeed, "the classifications of homosexual and heterosexual appeared at the same time that the United States began aggressively policing the borders between the United States and Mexico," with the creation of the Texas Rangers in the nineteenth century and the Border Patrol in 1924 (Pérez 2003, 126). From Yanelia's interaction with immigration officials, it is evident that the bodies and sexualities of migrants remain viewed as deviant. Sexuality, as it intersects with non-white status and assumed criminality, continues to affect possibilities for migrants to enter or remain in the United States as part of the shifting but ongoing process of keeping the nation free from "racial and sexual impurities" (Pérez 2003, 126).

LGBTQ migrant Latinas resisting: A journey toward home

In response to the violence perpetuated by the U.S. immigration system, informed by heteronormativity, exploitation, and white supremacy, the LGBTQ migrant Latina narrators in this article practice resistance. Their resistance offers possibilities to heal from migrating, fearing and facing deportation, lacking access to resources and protections, and the heteronormativity embedded in these processes. In other words, the narrators' resistance is oppositional to the systems that keep them marginalized. Resistance takes the form of daily survival, as well as engaging in community building and organizing. María Lugones's concept of inward subjectivity helps to illuminate their process. For Lugones, inward subjectivity, in contrast to the Western notion of agency, is "like a cocoon, the changes are not directed outward, at least not toward those domains permeated by the logics of domination," but are "more contained, more inward" (Lugones 2005, 86; Borges 2018). Inward subjectivity facilitates the narrators' ability to make their queer migrant lives livable under conditions of violence.

The narrators I interviewed in Los Angeles practiced daily survival while engaging in community building and organizing with other queer migrants of color. They grew up witnessing and experiencing firsthand how oppressive systems harm vulnerable populations. From these experiences, the narrators developed an inward process to survive and navigate relationships with family, which was also a source of strength to change norms and policy. Such processes are not linear, but instead intermesh with one another.

Imelda, for example, lived with her mother, siblings, and one aunt for years. She learned to navigate the realities of being working-class, undocumented, migrant, and queer under heteronormative, capitalist, and white supremacist structures. When she began to explore her queerness, she started presenting as more androgynous. Her aunt noticed what Imelda calls her masculine energy and would comment, "*¿Qué es eso? Te ves como un hombre*" (What is that? You look like a man). Imelda's response was:

> I try to laugh about it because I'm like, okay, that's your stuff, I ain't tryna take that in, so I just laugh about it. I'm like, "*Usted quiérame como soy, tía. ¿Qué le importa que sea hombre o no?*" (You just love me the way I am, auntie. What do you care if I'm a man or not?). She would be like, "*Ay, tú*" (Oh, you). You know, señora… Mexican señora (Mexican older woman) [laughs].

Imelda was clear that her aunt's comments, as a "Mexican señora" living within heteropatriarchal norms, could be blunt. Yet, they maintained a loving relationship and supported one another while living in vulnerable conditions. Despite her aunt's comments, Imelda did not question her own queerness. Rather, she embraced her queer identity *and* her family, refusing to give up either. She also shared information about her queer identity with her brother:

> I told my brother. I felt comfortable telling him. I was like, "*Oh, es que me identifico como fluida, es como… umm… imagínate bisexual pero diferente.*" You know? (Oh, I identify as fluid, it's like… umm… it's like bisexual, but different). You're trying to explain that and not just be like, "*soy jota*" (I'm queer) [laughs].

During Imelda's conversation with her brother, she navigated language and culture, wishing she could have simply said "*soy jota*," in Spanish, without needing to use Western identity labels that did not fit. A key element that allowed Imelda to embrace family and queerness was building community and organizing with other queer people of color. These experiences gave her the tools to navigate her aunt's comments, the lack of accessible language to communicate with her brother, and conceptualizations of gender and sexuality that were not Western. For instance, she learned about the term "two-spirit," specific to Indigenous communities, from close friends. She described two-spirit as "a Native understanding of queer identity that was beautiful to me and I understood." For Imelda, being queer, or "*jota*," from a Native understanding is:

> A blessing, a gift, being able to have different perspectives of the world, different understandings because you're not meant to be a part of a hetero-understanding of life. You're able to perceive and live life in a different way. And that's beautiful.

The way in which Imelda identified changed according to time and space. During conversations with her brother, her friends, and in our own interview, she defined herself in ways that seemed appropriate in those particular moments, but which can and do change. Understanding identity as something that changes rather than being static requires that we, as Carlos Decena (2011, 8) proposes, "capture 'being' as a movement without end, as enabling transitivity." In this context, sexuality, for Imelda, is a "movement without end." She further reflected:

> Being able to learn and acknowledge that by learning about two-spirited people, I felt like I began to understand myself better. I could connect to my spirituality…. It just felt like home.

Imelda's feeling at home in her own queerness contradicts systemic exclusion based on being a migrant, unauthorized, working-class, and a self-identified queer woman of color. She finds a sense of socio- and political belonging in her queerness, enabling her to resist oppression. Her journey to feeling at home in her queerness was also a journey to her spirituality. In *Fleshing the Spirit*, Irene Lara and Elisa Facio argue that attempts to control the sexuality of Chicana, Latina, and/or Indigenous women are inseparable from "control over spirituality." Therefore, "resistance, healing, and transformation of such oppression must engage both" (10). They further contend, "the claiming of their spirituality goes hand in hand with a deep sense of respect for and accountability to their communities" (4). Imelda, Anabel, and Claudia demonstrate this accountability to their communities in their organizing, which at the same time serves to create a sense of belonging for themselves.

Anabel exemplified her commitment to queer communities of color by asking:

> What's pressing in the community? This feeling of being useful in the community is home for me. What am I doing that's useful? Not only for me, but also [for the] people that live around me, people that have lived here for a long time.

Anabel has worked closely with and for women, queer, and trans low-income communities of color in Oakland and Los Angeles, California, doing reproductive justice and radical sex education. She has also organized against prisons, gentrification, and the criminalization of racialized communities in Los Angeles. Through organizing, Anabel created a community, building spaces where she can heal with others who are also targets of intersecting oppressions. Being in communities with queer people of color who are invested in radical change offered a source of strength under circumstances of family separation and marginalization in the United States. It was integral to her survival, and made her life livable. It allowed her to "be real" with herself. She continues to organize, writes blogs, and gives workshops on reproductive justice and healing from radical, non-Western, non-binary, and non-heteropatriarchal lenses.

In Imelda's case, when I asked if she seeks out queer spaces, she firmly responded, "I don't seek out queer spaces, I feel *like I create queer spaces*" (emphasis mine). Imelda explained it is not easy to find spaces that are exclusively for undocumented queer people. For that reason, she and two close friends who, at that time, shared these social locations "started looking further for other undocumented folks." They began creating spaces that would become identified as "undocuqueer." The term "undocuqueer" is credited to artist and activist Julio Salgado, who called "attention to the unique situation of queers in the migrant rights movement" (Chávez 2013, 81), and specifically to undocumented queer migrants:

> The three of us kind of started organizing and doing undocuqueer work around the Pomona/La Puente area [California]. Eventually, we found out about other folks who were organizing with undocuqueers in Orange County. It's been difficult to find *mujeres* [women], so, [I'm] trying to create queer undocumented *mujer* [woman] spaces, at least migrant *mujer* spaces. You're not gonna find those.

Imelda's undocuqueer organizing was intimately intertwined with her healing process, and she was clear that her community building and organizing needed to take place with other undocuqueers, not in white LGBTQ spaces:

> With a lot of the work that I do, I think it's beautiful because it's allowed me to meet some pretty dope [great] people, some very beautiful people. And so I've been fortunate to be in spaces with queer people of color in general, which has been very beautiful, feeling very at home. I feel uncomfortable around white queers and those spaces just don't feel like... you know [...]. Their conversations are different. What is pressing and significant in our lives doesn't... We're struggling to survive, struggling to defend ourselves, build[ing] protections in different ways, as opposed to build[ing] on privileges.

The type of home that Imelda is referencing is one outside nationalist and heteronormative markers, and that pushes against and challenges the structures that keep queer migrants isolated: immigration and criminalization systems, heteropatriarchal and heteronormative ideologies, and economic, political, and physical borders. In other words, these spaces did not only provide possibilities for organizing but for a kind of belonging that made survival possible.[5] Both organizing and survival depended on and fed each other as undocuqueer visibility grew out of a context of oppression.

Claudia, also an organizer, explained that she was also seeking spaces that were undocumented and queer. It was not possible for her to separate the two, to split herself in half. As self-defined undocuqueers, Imelda, Claudia, and others employed critiques and strategies that differed from mainstream movements and narratives. These dominant narratives prioritized gay marriage as the ultimate gay liberation and the DREAM (Development, Relief, and Education for Alien Minors) Act as progressive immigration reform. The DREAM Act was first introduced in Congress in 2001 but has never passed; it constructed DREAMers as undocumented youth who were brought by their parents as children to, and attended school in, the United States, portraying them as productive members of society who could not have known that they were breaking immigration law (Nair 2011). In 2013, at an event at the Gay and Lesbian Center in Los Angeles, undocuqueer activists, including Claudia and Imelda, offered critiques of the Dreamer narrative as one that portrays undocumented students as exceptional and pits immigrants against each other, and of gay marriage as focused on binational couples. Both narratives, they pointed out, ignore the criminalization of family members, including parents, who might also be undocumented (field notes). An undocuqueer panelist identified one of their goals as "to go beyond marriage equality and migration rights." At the same time, Claudia explained in our interview that she does not judge people who use the institution of marriage to get *some* protection. For Claudia, it was possible to have both a critical analysis of marriage equality as a reductionist activist strategy and compassion for migrants who are able to use it for survival.

"Why do you think Undocuqueers wanna do a lot of healing?": Healing from violence

The narrators' resistance is further evidenced in their stance on the need for healing. For them, it is not enough to recognize systemic oppression and be involved in activism because, without healing from violence, activism is neither possible nor sustainable. The three narrators in Los Angeles in particular approached violence from a healing standpoint. Imelda spoke about doing activism for over ten years, time during which "continuing to push [her] body has made [her] very sick." Anabel, too, sees the deterioration of oppressed populations' health as a direct result of violence and marginalization. From her lens as a queer migrant, she characterizes migration as "really painful; very unhealthy, super unhealthy." Furthermore, Imelda's experiences with migration and mainstream LGBT organizing give her a perspective to understand the immediate need for undocuqueers to heal:

> [I'm] just doing health work because that's also very real.[…] I started organizing around resources for healing, for healing-justice spaces, speaking on sustainability of our movement, on emotional wellness, the psychological battle that we're losing as undocumented people and the need to support each other in that sense, emotionally, so that we're able to recognize our strength, building empowerment with each other. All of that comes through talking and discussions, which in academic spaces we've address as the emotional and psychological wellness. But within our communities, it's much more than that. It's more about sustainability. It's about our overall health, the difference between living and surviving our lives, our self-worth. Being able to recognize that we are worthy and entitled to be better than any reform is offering, so we should be able to demand better.

The process of healing for Imelda is not an individual task. The act of healing in community disrupts historical and ongoing patterns of oppression that make marginalized people ill. In "The American Indian Holocaust: Healing Historical Unresolved Grief," Maria Yellow Horse Brave Heart and Lemyra M. DeBruyn (1997, 75) analyze the historical trauma of Native Americans populations, arguing that "community healing along with individual and family healing are necessary to thoroughly address historical unresolved grief and in present manifestations." Indigenous two-spirit scholar Megan MacDonald (2010) further proposes the need for closed healing spaces for two-spirit peoples. While the contexts are different, and specificities must not be flattened, the need for healing in community for the narrators in this article is apparent.

In Claudia's view, it is no coincidence that LGBTQ migrants of color do healing work. Specifically speaking of undocuqueers, she states:

> I feel like a lot of undocuqueers were doing a lot of healing work 'cause we have to, for ourselves. A friend of mine was telling us, you know, when we come from all these interesting identities, it's like, we have to do a lot of healing. A *lot* of healing. That's why it's like, why are you surprised that undocuqueers wanna do a lot of healing work? [...] I know a lot of other [immigrant] organizations are not worried about healing. It comes with queer identity, too. It's a different perspective.

There was no question for Claudia that undocuqueers needed to actively do healing work as part of their organizing efforts and everyday lives. She understood that, as people who are targeted by multiple systems of power, healing practices are urgent to avoid premature illness and death. In *Queer Necropolitics*, Jin Haritaworn, Adi Kuntsman, and Silvia Posocco (2014, 4) discuss the ways in which queers who are racialized and Othered undergo forms of "killing and of 'letting die.'" By theorizing queer necropolitics, the authors argue that "everyday death worlds" range from "war, torture or imperial invasion" to "completely normalized violence," which include "the disposing and abandonment of others" (2). Undocuqueers and other LGBTQ migrants, as racialized, exploited, disposable, and forgotten populations, see the healing of their communities as a radical act against violence. It not only centers survival, but also, and especially, *living*.

Conclusion

Closely engaging feminisms of color, queer of color critique, and queer migration studies allows me to use a multi-lens framework that reveals the complexity of LGBTQ migrant Latinas' relationship to state violence and resistance. This framework helps us to understand the narratives of LGBTQ migrant Latinas, uncovering the depth of violence that the state re/produces against them while highlighting the resistance that the narrators practice in their daily lives. In this article, I therefore complicate mainstream scholarship that largely uses single-axis or additive frameworks in its analysis of oppression and liberation. The multi-lens framework I employ exposes the continuous struggle of LGBTQ migrant Latinas to navigate and survive constant policing, disposability, and lack of access to resources. The structural hurdles to survival are created by systems that were never built to serve them. However, the narrators challenge this setup of having to continually fight for survival by practicing community building, activism, and healing. Healing from violence is crucial in challenging systems of oppression, especially in the face of social abandonment and early death of LGBTQ migrants of color.

The LGBTQ migrant Latina narrators in this article tell their stories of resistance, imagining and creating possibilities for healing and living. They tell these stories in their own words, their own ways, and in their own terms. Their healing is imperative to their resistance as narrators who not merely exist, but actively create the conditions for livable lives. By engaging in resistance, these LGBTQ migrant Latinas find powerful ways to define themselves, transform their experiences, and resist violence.

Notes

1. I use the broad term "Latina" to refer to women of Latin American descent who live, or have lived, in the United States.
2. Mexican queer migrant. I use the Spanish word "Mexicana" as a political act to reclaim Spanish to define my social location.
3. The estimate for LGBT-identified documented immigrants was 637,000 (Gates 2013, 2).
4. In September 2017, the Trump administration announced that the Department of Homeland Security (DHS) would begin collecting social media information from migrants, including permanent residents and naturalized citizens, to investigate possible criminal and terrorist affiliations. However, the *New York Times* documented that social media data had already been collected during the Obama administration (Nixon 2017). The difference, according to these sources, is that DHS had collected public information only. By accessing social media, immigration officials have been able to, long before 2017, determine suitability not only based on migrants' files, but also on information from social media accounts.

5. Scholars have addressed the role that home plays in the lives of queer migrants in the diaspora (Fortier 2001; Ahmed et al. 2003; Gopinath 2005; Borges 2018). Gayatri Gopinath argues that the migrant home is often constructed in nationalist, heterosexist, and patriarchal ways. Elsewhere, I propose to conceptualize the process of LGBTQ migrants creating homes of survival, or homing, as a form of protest.

References

Ahmed, Sara, Claudia Castañeda, Anne-Marie Fortier, and Mimi Sheller, eds. 2003. *Uprootings/Regroundings: Questions of Home and Migration*. Oxford, England: Berg Publishers.

Borges, Sandibel. 2018. "Home and Homing as Resistance: The Survival of LGBTQ Latinx Migrants." *Women's Studies Quarterly* 46 (3 and 4): 69–84.

Brave Heart, Maria Yellow Horse and Lemyra M. DeBruyn. 1997. "The American Indian Holocaust: Healing Historical Unresolved Grief." *American Indian and Alaska Native Mental Health Research* 8 (2): 60–82.

Butler, Judith. 1999. *Gender Trouble: Feminism and the Subversion of Identity*. New York, NY: Routledge.

Chang, Grace. 2016. *Disposable Domestics: Immigrant Women Workers in the Global Economy*, 2nd ed. Chicago, IL: Haymarket Books.

Chávez, Karma R. 2011. "Identifying the Needs of LGBTQ Immigrants and Refugees in Southern Arizona." *Journal of Homosexuality* 58 (2): 189–218.

Chávez, Karma R. 2013. *Queer Migration Politics: Activist Rhetoric and Coalitional Possibilities*. Urbana, IL: University of Illinois Press.

Decena, Carlos Ulises. 2011. *Tacit Subjects: Belonging and Same-Sex Desire among Dominican Immigrant Men*. Durham, NC: Duke University Press.

Driskill, Qwo-Li, Chris Finley, Brian Joseph Gilley, and Scott Lauria Morgensen, eds. 2011. *Queer Indigenous Studies: Critical Interventions in Theory, Politics, and Literature*. Tucson, AZ: The University of Arizona Press.

Facio, Elisa and Irene Lara, eds. 2014. *Fleshing the Spirit: Spirituality and Activism in Chicana, Latina, and Indigenous Women's Lives*. Tucson, AZ: The University of Arizona Press.

Fischer, Amelia. 2013. "Secure Communities, Racial Profiling, and Suppression Law in Removal Proceedings." *Texas Hispanic Journal of Law and Policy* 19 (1): 63–94.

Fortier, Anne-Marie. 2001. "'Coming Home.'" *European Journal of Cultural Studies* 4 (4): 405–424.

Gates, Gary J. *LGBT Adult Immigrants in the United States*. Los Angeles, CA: The Williams Institute, UCLA School of Law, 2013.

Gopinath, Gayatri. 2005. *Impossible Desires: Queer Diasporas and South Asian Public Cultures*. Durham, NC: Duke University Press.

Haritaworn, Jin, Adi Kuntsman, and Silvia Posocco, eds. 2014. *Queer Necropolitics*. New York, NY: Routledge.

Lugones, María. 2005. "From within Germinative Stasis: Creating Active Subjectivity, Resisting Agency." In *Entre Mundos: New Perspectives on Gloria E. Anzaldúa*, edited by Ana Louise Keating, 85–99. New York, NY: Palgrave MacMillan.

Luibhéid, Eithne. 2002. *Entry Denied: Controlling Sexuality at the Border*. Minneapolis, MN: University of Minnesota Press.

Luibhéid, Eithne. 2005. "Introduction: Queering Migration and Citizenship." In *Queer Migrations: Sexuality, U.S. Citizenship, and Border Crossings*, edited by Eithne Luibhéid and Lionel Cantú, xi–xlvi. Minneapolis, MN: University of Minnesota Press.

Luibhéid, Eithne. 2008. "Queer/Migration: An Unruly Body of Scholarship." *GLQ: A Journal of Lesbian and Gay Studies* 14 (2–3): 168–190.

MacDonald, Megan L. 2010. "Two Spirit Organizing: Indigenous Two-Spirit Identity in the Twin Cities Region." In *Queer Twin Cities: Twin Cities GLBT Oral History Project*, edited by Twin Cities GLBT Oral History Project, 150–170. Minneapolis, MN: University of Minnesota Press.

Muñoz, José Esteban. 1999. *Disidentifications: Queers of Color and the Performance of Politics*. Minneapolis, MN: University of Minnesota Press.

Muñoz, José Esteban. 2009. *Cruising Utopia: The Then and There of Queer Futurity*. New York, NY: New York University Press.

Nair, Yasmine. 2011. "How to Make Prisons Disappear: Queer Immigrants, the Shackle of Love, and the Invisibility of the Prison Industrial Complex." In *Captive Genders: Trans Embodiment and the Prison Industrial Complex*, edited by Eric A. Stanley and Nat Smith, 123–140. Edinburgh, Scotland: AK Press.

Naples, Nancy A. and Salvador Vidal-Ortiz, eds. 2009. *The Sexuality of Migration: Border Crossings and Mexican Immigrant Men*. New York, NY: New York University Press.

Nixon, Ron. 2017. "U.S. to Collect Social Media Data on All Immigrants Entering the Country." *New York Times*, September 28. https://www.nytimes.com/2017/09/28/us/politics/immigrants-social-media-trump.html.

Pérez, Emma. 2003. "Queering the Borderlands: The Challenges of Excavating the Invisible and Unheard." *Frontiers: A Journal of Women's Studies* 24 (2 and 3): 122–131.

Romero, Mary. 2006. "Racial Profiling and Immigration Law Enforcement: Rounding Up of Usual Suspects in the Latino Community." *Critical Sociology* 32 (2–3): 447–473.

Simanski, John and Lesley M. Sapp. *Immigration Enforcement Actions: 2011*. Washington, DC: Office of Immigration Statistics, U.S. Department of Homeland Security, 2012.

Somerville, Siobhan. 1994. "Scientific Racism and the Emergence of the Homosexual Body." *Journal of the History of Sexuality* 5 (2): 243–266.

U.S. Citizenship and Immigration Services. n.d. "Voluntary Departure." U.S. Department of Homeland Security. https://www.uscis.gov/ilink/docView/FR/HTML/FR/0-0-0-1/0-0-0-102229/0-0-0-106136/0-0-0-106514/0-0-0-106604.html.

Zavella, Patricia. 2011. *I'm Neither Here nor There: Mexicans' Quotidian Struggles with Migration and Poverty*. Durham, NC: Duke University Press.

ə OPEN ACCESS

Challenging the visibility paradigm: Tracing ambivalences in lesbian migrant women's negotiations of sexual identity

Mia Liinason

ABSTRACT
In this article, I want to illuminate a more diverse image of lesbian lives in the Nordic region than what is often assumed through Western-centric notions of the global queer community and of "out and proud" visibility. Moving beyond dichotomous divisions between visibility and invisibility, I approach in/visibility as an ambivalent, ambiguous, and performative concept. My fieldwork data illuminate that non-heterosexual migrant women in this context do not primarily subscribe to a so-called "Western" visibility paradigm. I analyze how non-heterosexual migrant women, primarily Muslim, exercise ownership of their sexual identities and how they negotiate the degree to which their romantic and sexual relations become—or do not—points of discussion. As these women were involved in multi-layered negotiations in relation to their families, queer communities, and nations, their positionings in relation to the visibility paradigm differed. However, on a general level, their positionings could be interpreted as simultaneously in and out of the closet, or neither in nor out. These ambivalences and ambiguities, I suggest, illuminate the need to challenge the visibility/invisibility divide, and highlight the importance of paying attention to multiple, context-specific, and intersecting forms of power. Drawing on these discussions, I propose the need to rethink notions of community, family, and home within a framework of queer livability.

Introduction

This article addresses the complex dynamics that characterize the negotiations of sexual identity among non-heterosexual migrant women, located within multiple relations of power that are structured by gender, sexuality, ethnicity, race, religion, and national belonging. Drawing on ethnographic fieldwork with staff and members of organizations that work to support lgbti people with minority background in Denmark and Norway, I explore and problematize the visibility/

This is an Open Access article distributed under the terms of the Creative Commons Attribution-NonCommercial-NoDerivatives License (http://creativecommons.org/licenses/by-nc-nd/4.0/), which permits non-commercial re-use, distribution, and reproduction in any medium, provided the original work is properly cited, and is not altered, transformed, or built upon in any way.

coming out paradigm within a context of lesbian Muslim and migrant activism in the Nordic countries. Showing how practices and discourses of in/visibility interact with homonationalist agendas, the analyses in this article makes explicit the ways in which such agendas promote homotolerance as a national value in the Nordic region at the same time that homophobia is projected onto racialized people and migrant populations (Akin 2019). As a result, non-heterosexual Muslim migrant women are produced in contradictory ways as both "impossible and un-imaginable" (Gopinath 2005: 16) and simultaneously hyper-visible and invisible. Yet, I also want to challenge assumptions that the "majority" has the sole power to categorize people into visible or invisible, by acknowledging that minorities also have influence over their own practices of in/visibility, which may tactically be used for their advantage (Leinonen and Toivanen 2014). In what follows, I seek to illuminate a more diverse image of lesbian lives in the Nordic region than what is often assumed through Western-centric notions of the global queer community and of "out and proud" visibility. I aim to do this by examining how non-heterosexual migrant women, primarily Muslim, in Norway and Denmark exercise ownership of their sexual identities and negotiate the degree to which their romantic and sexual relations become—or do not—points of discussion.

My analysis is inspired by postcolonial feminist and queer of color scholarship that has contributed nuanced understandings of non-heterosexual or non-heteronormative desires, practices, identifications, and embodiments (Manalansan 1997; Luibhéid 2014; Gopinath 2005, 2018; Decena 2008; Peumans 2014; Shakhsari 2014; Stella 2015). As I will show, for the queer migrant women in my fieldwork data, the family and the home emerge as multifaceted sites of struggle. Their non-heterosexual embodiments and practices are not easily captured within a logic of visibility. Rather, following Carlos Ulises Decena's notion of "tacit subjects" (2008: 339), I argue that it is more fruitful to understand these enactments as inhabiting a space which is simultaneously in and out of the closet, or neither in nor out, in unstable and sometimes contradictory ways, and I propose that these dynamics highlight the need to rethink notions of community, home, and family within a framework of queer livability.

While these ambivalences and ambiguities confirm findings in previous studies, the discussion in this article seeks to deepen our understandings of how non-heterosexual migrant women negotiate such dynamics within the context of the family and the home, as well as within the queer community and the nation. In light of the fact that most research of queer Muslims has focused on gay men, I hope that my analysis can contribute important understanding of everyday enactments of sexual identities of migrant lesbian women within and beyond a dominant coming-out paradigm, problematizing dichotomous divisions between public/private and visibility/invisibility.

Note on terminology

In lgbti activism and queer studies, issues of language and representation are crucial sites of struggle and transformation. In the title, I use the gendered term "lesbian" to highlight gender as an important part of the experiences of non-heterosexual women included in my fieldwork; however, to illuminate the variety of women's experiences, practices and identifications, I use the terms non-heterosexual, as well as bisexual and lesbian women, throughout the article. Moreover, I use "gay" as a collective term for non-heterosexual people. The term was frequently used by my research participants, which is the main reason why I use it in this article. Unlike gay, "queer" has been translated in different ways to the languages of the region. In Norway, the word *skeiv* is used, while the Danish and Swedish languages have adopted the Anglo-American term *queer* to their languages and recent histories. Scholars caution of the risks of queer becoming "too popular" and depoliticized (Dahl 2009: 145; Bolsø 2008). Notably, some of my research participants preferred expressions like "person I fall in love with," rather than claiming universalized identity categories such as lesbian, bisexual, gay, or queer. Furthermore, as an overarching term, for example when referring to particular NGOs, I use the abbreviation lgbti (lesbian, gay, bisexual, transgender, and intersex), since that is the term used by the organizations. I use it with lowercase letters to support readability. The categories "Muslim" and "migrant" should not be read as mutually exclusive, but as simultaneously overlapping and multiple. I use "migrant" to refer to the experience of crossing an international border for reasons other than tourism, and "second- or third-generation migrant" to refer to people whose parents, or grandparents, have had this experience.

Theoretical frame

While much queer scholarship on in/visibility tends to reproduce universalist constructions of a global queer community and sustain expectations of visibility for authentic or "true" gayness, in this article I have been inspired by postcolonial feminist and queer of color scholarship that attempts to push the discussion beyond dichotomous divisions of visibility/invisibility, and bring to light intersecting dynamics that structure non-conforming bodies, desires, and affiliations. Processes of in/visibility are uneven and diverse, embedded in homonationalist logics of recognition as well as in homo- and Islamophobic discourses. I suggest that an analytic focus on "how certain groups and individuals become 'visible' or 'invisible'—for example, in daily encounters with persons representing the 'majority'"—can shed light on broader processes of racialization in a Nordic context (Leinonen and Toivanen 2014: 161). My theoretical approach to in/visibility in this article is based on three key arguments. First, I understand visibility and invisibility as ambivalent concepts, connected to complex processes of claiming recognition and rights within the racist and capitalist logics of nation-states (White 2013). Visibility and invisibility are charged with ambivalence, shaping "negative" and "positive" forms of visibility, oscillating between hypervisibility—visibility—invisibility (Leinonen and Toivanen 2014; Luibhéid 2014). Second, negotiations of in/visibility express ambiguities that make explicit that visibility and invisibility should not be understood as mutually exclusive, but rather as co-existent in complex ways. These ambiguities capture tensions inherent to gendered, sexualized, and racialized positions defined by homonationalist agendas. Such tensions are not limited to migrants or refugees, but at work in the positions of racialized and queer groups in general (Sager 2018; McNevin 2009; Peumans 2014). Third, in/visibility has a performative dimension; for instance, in the case of "aesthetic forms, dress codes, or architectural genres" (Göle 2011: 387), which allows for a sensitivity to agency in the analysis of positions of in/visibility. That is the case, for example, when groups make claims for greater public visibility, or attempt to control the public image of certain populations, or when groups seek to remain invisible from public attention (Leinonen and Toivanen 2014).

In *Impossible Desires*, Gopinath (2005: 14) develops a crucial intervention into postcolonial feminist and queer scholarly understandings of the "home." Differently from existing understandings of the home as primarily a site of "gender and sexual oppression for female and queer subjects," as a place to be escaped and left behind for another "more liberatory" space, Gopinath shows that queer migrant racialized subjects may be more concerned with "remaking the space of home from within" (2005: 14, 15), such that "'staying put' becomes a way of remaining within the oppressive structures of the home—as a domestic space, racialized community space and national space—while imaginatively working to dislodge its heteronormative logic."

Influenced by Gopinath's rich theorization of remaking the space of home from within—the family, the community, the nation—I provide a reading of the narratives of family, home, and the queer community expressed by lesbian migrant women in Denmark and Norway, bringing to light the important role of affective ties, emergent from collective frameworks of everyday experience. In these frameworks of everyday experience, as I will show, resistance is expressed through collective forms of action, carving out spaces for queer livability within multiple constraints.

I have found Carlos Ulises Decena's notion about tacit subjects fruitful to illustrate the "complicities that constitute social relations" (2008: 355). Similar to Decena (2008), I found my research participants expressing an ambiguity in their positioning as simultaneously in and out, or neither in nor out, and in what follows, I will explore how these ambiguities are expressed in the negotiations of sexual identity and home among non-heterosexual migrant women (Esack and Mahomed 2011).

Research that challenges notions of essentialized place and homogenous identity provides useful frames for a critical engagement with variations across space and scale. Francesca Stella (2015) uses the concept of critical regionalism as an analytic frame to capture variations across different spatial scales (e.g., the nation, urban locales, the body). Moreover, attending to the region as a "minor" site and location of "queer possibility" (2018: 6), Gopinath highlights the multiscalar potentiality of critical regionalism, able to "disturb and disrupt the inherited colonial and neocolonial cartographies keeping differently racialized bodies, as well as histories of displacement and dispossession, segregated and discrete" (2018: 17). These understandings provide useful insights for my analysis, illuminating how locally anchored and multiscalar but also transnationally connected relationships build spaces for Muslim and/or migrant queer livability within places and relations with multiple constraints.

Previous research on non-heterosexual migrant women has emphasized the difficulties resulting from the so-called double invisibility of migrant lesbian women (Avrahami 2007), and highlighted feelings of isolation among Muslim lesbian women (Siraj 2011). I am more interested in examining enactments of resistance to gain deeper insights around how expressions of in/visibility work performatively and how collective action in grassroots organizations can create conditions that make spaces livable. I also want to learn more about how the refusals among lesbian migrant women to comply with the normative expectations of being "out and proud" can be understood as resistances against contextually embedded expectations of certain forms of gendered, ethnicized, racialized, and religious identities in this context. I have been inspired by Eithne Luibhéid's (2014) insistence on the multiple ways in which minorities, such as queer migrants, not only experience difficulties as the result of certain expectations on identity categories, but also have the possibility to trouble and transform those categories as a result of their presence and everyday actions. Building further on these insights, my findings suggest the need to challenge the visibility/invisibility dichotomy in scholarship and activism, and highlight the importance of paying attention to multiple, context-specific, and intersecting forms of power and subjectivity.

Race, nationhood, and homotolerance in the Nordic context

Scholars demonstrate how ideologies of racelessness in the Nordic countries historically and presently have functioned to make migrants and racialized groups invisible as participants in the labor market and in social and cultural spheres, at the same time that these groups have been exposed to a kind of hypervisibilization through "stigmatizing, criminalizing and/or victimizing representations" (Sager 2018: 176; Liinason 2018a; Leinonen and Toivanen 2014; Loftsdóttir and Jensen 2016). While these developments in the Nordic countries have distinct characteristics (Mulinari et al. 2009), such historical erasures and present exclusions are not unique to the Nordic context, but part of a broader pattern that is repeated throughout Europe (El-Tayeb 2012). Meanwhile, since the early 2000s, a narrative of the Nordic countries as homotolerant has been growing. This narrative is presented by various actors, from welfare institutions and representatives of trade and industry, to politicians and civil society actors. Currently, homotolerance is referred to as a national value and in different ways used in geopolitical positioning strategies in relation to other, seemingly less homotolerant, countries and regions. Simultaneously, within the Nordic countries, homophobia is increasingly projected onto racialized and migrant populations (Akin 2019), as Islamophobic and Orientalist discourses are utilized by conservative, far right and Christian parties and movements, spreading a more or less explicit nationalist ideology connecting Whiteness, national belonging, and Christianity/secularity with agendas of gender equality and homotolerance. Moreover, since the emergence of the so-called war on terror, and similar to many other regions in the global West, the concept of "migrant" often becomes equated with stereotypical images of "Muslims" (Leinonen and Toivanen 2014: 163). These Islamophobic and homonationalist discourses work at a supra-national level to reinforce global power hierarchies by locating the Nordic countries at the forefront of planetary development. Simultaneously, they work at sub-national levels to obscure the various ways in which the everyday life of non-heterosexual migrants is experienced. While racialized citizens are "permanently treated as 'immigrants'" (Sager 2018: 176), the colonial legacies of the Nordic countries, as well as the various historical forms of racisms in these countries, are frequently erased from national memory (Keskinen et al. 2009; Liinason 2018b). In this context, drawing on fieldwork with refugee, migrant, Muslim, and racialized lgbti people, I use the concept of livability as an open, explorative concept to learn from my research contexts what makes, and could make, everyday spaces livable for lgbti people. In using the concept of livability, I have been inspired by the transnational Making Liveable Lives project, run by a collective of activists and scholars in India and the UK (see Browne et al. 2017). My motivations for exploring livability rather than rights are anchored in the self-description of many of my research participants, who do not see themselves as conducting political work. In addition, my research participants—who are Muslim queers; queer

Indigenous people; and lesbian, gay, or trans people of color with migrant experience—describe that they encounter suspicion, discrimination, hate speech, and violence from such diverse actors as state authorities, teachers, potential employers, and members of the community. Given these dynamics, contingent on divisions between worthy and not-worthy lgbti subjects within homonationalist agendas (Alinia 2011; Puar 2007; Spivak 2004), I find the notion of livability fruitful. Livability highlights the tension between openness and stability in recognition through identity categories (Butler 2004; Biswas et al. 2016) in a way that I believe better can support my attempt to sustain an open-ended reflection around the conditions and relations that make lives livable, rather than secure categories of identity.

Methodology and material

I conducted multi-sited fieldwork in 2017 and 2018 with more than ten local, national, and transnational lgbti organizations and groups in Denmark, Norway, Sweden, Belgium, and Spain. My data consist of fieldwork diaries from participant observation at events, seminars, courses, and get-togethers arranged by the groups over a period of one and a half years, and twenty in-depth interviews with staff and members of the organizations and groups. Most of the research participants have experience of migration, as first or second generation; many are people of color; and some are racialized as Black. From this larger body of material, I offer a close reading of fieldwork data collected in encounters with two lgbti organizations that work to strengthen the position of lgbti minorities in Denmark and Norway: Sabaah and Queer World (Skeiv Verden).

The organizations receive funding from local government budgets, but also rely extensively on volunteers. Each has headquarters in the capital cities of Copenhagen and Oslo, respectively, and subdivisions in other parts of the countries. Sabaah was established in 2006 in Copenhagen and today organizes social, cultural, and political activities for lgbti people with minority backgrounds. In 2010, Queer World was established as an organization independent from the national Norwegian lgbti organization FRI—Foreningen for kjønns- og seksualitetsmangfold [Association for Gender and Sexuality Diversity]. Both Queer World and Sabaah are connected to the European Queer Muslim network coordinated by Maruf in the Netherlands. The transnational nature of these groups challenges the nation-state as the given frame of reference and realm of action, and instead points to a multiplicity of communities and geographies. In that way, these transnational exchanges shape new cartographies of connectivity across regions with the potential to challenge, or even bypass, the nation-state (Gopinath 2018).

In addition to community building activities, Sabaah and Queer World offer counseling for individual users or groups, and organize events, such as workshops, for members on topics like worker's rights, sex education, sexual rights, or asylum rights, giving users the "skills to take up the fights in their own communities," as Minoo, a staff member of Sabaah, formulates it. They also organize events like panel discussions for the general public or conferences with politicians and other NGOs and arrange courses for social workers, teachers, and health care professionals on topics like intersectionality or living conditions for people who are "double minorities." Aspiring to become more inclusive for lesbian, bi-, and trans minority women, both organizations arrange separatist cafés, only open for female-identified people. They have taken different actions to create a safe space in the organizations; Sabaah, for instance, uses gender non-binary language and has begun to locate meetings at a "secret" address in the city center, scheduled in the afternoons instead of evenings.

I draw on seven in-depth interviews with staff members and members of both organizations, and field diaries from seven events within the organizations, including engaging in leisure activities such as cooking and eating dinner together; relaxed gathering in the headquarters in preparations for Oslo Pride; and taking part in workshops, seminars, and conferences. One of these events, a workshop on intimacy and love for lgbti people with minority backgrounds, stretched across three days. Another event, a conference with politicians on religion, ethnicity, gender identity, and sexuality, lasted one full day; but, in most cases, the events lasted two to four hours. Attending to the ambivalences and ambiguities inherent in the narratives of non-heterosexual migrant women in these contexts, I attempt to illuminate the multiplicity of power relations involved and connect these to the Nordic region. Paying attention to the varieties, overlaps, and fluidities between multiple scales—in this case, the family, the home, the queer community, and the nation—I hope to contribute to a nuanced understanding of place and identity beyond universalizing categories and Western-centric assumptions.

The visibility paradigm: Negotiations and resistances

In my interactions with staff and members of these organizations, issues of coming out or being open about one's sexual orientation were often brought up. Initially, at gatherings, when I encountered what I understood as celebratory narratives around the possibilities offered in the Nordic countries for living visibly as gay, often presented by migrant men, I reacted with a certain amount of skepticism, relating to my own ambivalent experience as a bisexual Swedish woman who experienced a continuous silencing of the issue from family and friends, resulting in struggles with myself around in/authenticity. The encounters with these celebratory narratives brought painful memories to the surface, feeding into a hierarchy between those who have come out and those who have not (Strømsvik 2017). One early entry in my field diary suggests: "I sometimes feel that I am not a real bisexual woman because I am not always out about it. This means my identity isn't so often mirrored, challenged or confirmed by others. Expectations of openness makes me feel a pressure, as if my feelings are not enough."

As I became more deeply immersed into the field, I begun to reconsider those statements from an intersectional standpoint. While I had started off searching for parallels in the experiences of same-sex intimacies and non-normative sexualities among myself and the migrants in the organizations, I soon began to pay more attention to the differences between us, on the basis of gender, ethnicity, race, religion, and national belonging. In most of the leisure activities in which I took part, the majority of participants were refugee gay men, while a small number were genderqueer and gender non-binary refugees. In conversations and interviews, we frequently returned to the issue of visibility, and almost all of the men emphasized the importance of being open about being gay. For example, Abra, a 21-year-old refugee man from Syria, said in an interview: "If I am not open about being gay, it means I am ashamed of it. I am not ashamed of it—it is the one thing I am proud of!" An intersectional analysis, paying attention to entanglements among gender, sexuality, ethnicity/race, religion, and national belonging, suggests that such expressions of visibility should be understood as negotiating dominant images of sexual minorities in the Nordic countries, rather than negotiating the limitations of the closet. As Deniz Akin (2017) suggests, such negotiations can take quite complex forms within contexts of NGO and community support, since mainstream gay and lesbian organizations often sustain dominant images. Expressions of visibility, Akin (2017) writes, could be understood as embracing a lifestyle previously denied, or a strategy to fit in to the new country, or a combination of both. In these ways, a narrative of visibility can be deployed by lgbti refugees in their fight for "becoming not only legible, but also desirable as a prospective citizen who will benefit the host society in the long run," adding credibility to their claims for asylum by referring to "authentic" forms of gender and sexuality (Akin 2017: 464; Shakhsari 2014). In this sense, expressions of visibility could be understood as negotiating dominant images of sexual minorities. Yet, at another level, these dynamics indicate the existence of a certain "gendering of queerness" (Strømsvik 2017: 11; Neufeld 2018; Siraj 2011), as non-heterosexual women in my fieldwork seldom subscribed to such coming out paradigms, while gay and bisexual men frequently did.

These dynamics points to the need for deeper explorations of how dominant images of sexual minorities work through the intersections between gender, sexuality, religion, and national belonging.

In/visibility: Ambivalence and ambiguity

Narratives of family, home, and community among non-heterosexual migrant women, primarily Muslim, which I encountered during fieldwork provided me with a nuanced understanding of the relationship between resistance and power (Abu-Lughod 1990), while shedding critical light on universalizing tropes of coming out, visibility, and authentic sexuality. In the narratives, coming out was not always perceived as necessary or empowering. This had partly to do with the role of the home, which in the women's narratives was constructed both as an intimate space and a place of everyday homophobia that was difficult to negotiate. Yet, home was sometimes also linked with wider society, as well as the queer community. Negotiations around coming out and visibility were especially present in the narratives of younger women who were studying and still living at home. Among these women, positions ranged from being unsure if they really were gay, to those who knew very well that they were gay and were living a double life, to women who were very open about it. For women over 30, the role of the family was less pervasive, as one of my interlocutors explained; it was still there, but questions around being gay in the workplace, how and if to talk about gayness at work, as well as questions of marriage and kids, were more central for those women.

Jasmin, a staff member of Sabaah, describes that most of their members now are open about their sexuality, although it varies. Many women have had numerous conflicts with their families, yet today, Jasmin describes, most have achieved some kind of peace with them. They are welcome in the home on the condition that "they don't talk about it":

> … at this moment, we don't have any [women here] who have broken off completely with their family. I know we have had. But at this moment, I don't think we have anyone who have broken it completely off. Somehow they manage to find a way to have a relationship. Sometimes they would have to compromise in a way that… is fine… and they just don't talk about it. We have some women who have gone so far as to introduce their girlfriends to their mothers but they won't say the word… they would say "my friend" and the mother would speak about them as "your friend." That's as far as we can go. It's some kind of acceptance.

However, silent acceptance did not always work, and some women felt abandoned by their mothers:

I feel frustrated because I feel like I have to write it in neon. I feel like I have put so many hints. But she [my mother] just don't pick up on it, until I utter the words "I am gay." She still doesn't understand, but she should know by now.

In these quotes, the home takes shape as a place of struggle, a place which the women tried to negotiate by giving hints but not explicitly saying that they were gay. When it worked, silent understanding enabled the women to bring their girlfriends home and introduce them to their parents. In those cases, visibility was not considered as an empowering act, but as jeopardizing the compromise and feeling of safety in the family. Yet, silent understanding did not always work, which led some women to feel misrecognized or abandoned by their mothers in frustrating and upsetting ways. In these situations, however, the women were aware that if they broke with their families, they would face other difficulties:

Jasmin: Being Brown in a very White country has its challenges. Being Muslim in a very secular and atheist society has its challenges, being lgbt in a heteronormative society… and then within [the queer community], there is Islamophobia and racism. There is even transphobia and sexism. So many levels of, you know, which spaces you feel welcome in.

Emphasizing that wider social relations are structured by power relationships on the basis of gender, sexuality, race, religion and national belonging that won't go away, Sabrina, a member of Sabaah, says straightforwardly: "There is no option to break with my family. It's not a solution to the problem."

Engaged in multi-layered negotiations around homophobia in the family, and racism and Islamophobia in the queer community and wider society, the narratives of these women illuminate that the choice of being out and proud is not "equally available to all queers" (Stella 2012: 1841). The tacit agreements in the family bring to light the fluidity of the border between visibility and invisibility, as these women were simultaneously in and out of the closet, or neither in nor out. For many of these women, lack of disclosure was more important than visibility, as it enabled a continued relationship with their families while, at the same time, they could be romantically involved, invite their girlfriends home, and introduce them for their parents. Being "neither secret or silent" (Decena 2008: 340), such tacit engagements can make a process of coming out redundant, as a verbal expression of what is already understood. Underlining the complicity of all involved in a public secret, "[k]nowing what not to know" becomes crucial in those tacit forms of understanding (Decena 2008: 345). These conversations suggest the potentiality of "staying put," while simultaneously seeking to displace heteronormativity from within (Gopinath 2005).

Given that negotiations around the closet always are embedded in particular social circumstances, both Decena (2008) and Stella (2015) propose reframing coming out not as an individual project and the result of personal choice, but as a collective process of identity formation. In such a collective process of identity negotiation, visibility is not always seen as an empowering act, and expressions of authentic sexuality are not necessarily desirable (Stella 2015). In many contexts, Stella emphasizes, group solidarity is important, as is the role of the collective in breaking isolation. My interlocutors emphasized similar dynamics.

Multifaceted sites of struggle

In further conversations with these organizations, I brought up the question of community, asking to what extent the queer community could be seen as a "chosen" family. Stressing that queer communities are regulated by gendered and racialized boundaries, Jasmin says:

> There are jokes about the organization being a family. But for most people we are not. We [the community] are also divided within. [...] The community is more than the organization, and the community is not always nice. It can never take the place of a family.

In a slightly more open-ended perspective, Lynne, who is a staff member at Queer World, explains, "The organization is like any other family, there are conflicts and struggles going on. That is what we have to work with."

From their different positionalities, both statements challenge the binary division between private and public, demonstrating that the queer community is a space traversed by affinities, close ties, and power relations of different kinds, and that their organizations are no exception. Illuminating the existence of oppressive relations and structures in all social contexts, these conversations highlight how staying put can dislodge the heteronormative, racist, or Islamophobic logics structuring social relation, to remake "the space of home from within" (Gopinath 2005: 14).

Rather than being based on naturalized conceptions of familial, cultural, or national belonging, these conversations show that affective ties and personal relationships can shape feelings of belonging (to a family, to a community, to a place). Such constructions of family and home are not necessarily free from power relations and need to be managed carefully and respectfully. Dana, a staff member of Queer World, says:

> To be someone's contact in a moment of emergency, to take these minutes and to answer the phone, is a very rare privilege. [...] I don't take that for granted. I can use [our close relationships] in a political struggle but I need to manage this very carefully so I don't appear with a quote in the first page of the newspaper, saying that Queer World needs more resources because there are so many that are calling us at night time. [...] It is a fine balance. I am a mentor, advisor, friend [in times of crisis]... and I am there also when things are going fine.

In the small space of the community in the organization, intimacy was expressed through feelings of loss and mourning but also happiness and joy, reflecting and creating "collective frameworks of memory" (Boym 1998). These dynamics illustrate that the parental home and the home of choice should not be understood as separate entities but as connected in specific ways, and sometimes the parental home and the home of choice are the same place (Stella 2015). Dana echoed that insight:

> I receive a lot of phone calls this time of the year [Christmas]. It is a heavy period we enter into. For the fifth year in a row, I will celebrate with Queer World. Others might suspect that I—as a lesbian and not fully Norwegian, who celebrates Christmas with someone other than my family—that my family doesn't accept me. That's not the case. […] Christmas with Queer World has meant that I survive a season when I usually feel sad and depressed. […] And in the end my father often comes along too.

By constructing family through affective ties, emergent from collective frameworks of everyday experience, this formation of home in the small space of the community in the organization challenged the racialized, sexualized, and gendered boundaries that regulated access to belonging in the wider queer community and society.

As these discussions show, resistance to dominant notions or expectations of sexual identities was not expressed through claims to visibility, a category fraught with deep ambivalences and rarely seen as empowering in itself, as it brought along multiple tensions related to the parental home and the community or society beyond the safer space in the home of choice. Rather, similar to Decena's and Stella's understanding of invisibility as an expression of "both accommodation and resistance to existing social norms" (Stella 2012: 1843; Decena 2008), resistance to normative expectations about sexual identities was expressed through collective action, challenging the borders between private/public and between visibility/invisibility, navigating the multiplicities of power as they were making space for livability within places and relations of multiple constraints.

Conclusion

In this article, I have considered the ways in which practices and discourses of in/visibility interact with agendas of homotolerance, Islamophobia, and homophobia, and attended to forms of resistance expressed against such relations of power. Influenced by an understanding of in/visibility as an ambivalent, ambiguous, and performative concept, I have explored how non-heterosexual migrant women negotiate sexual identities within contexts of family relations, home, and community. For these women, the home was not a place to be left behind for another, "more liberatory" space. Rather, they were "staying put" and remaking "the space of home from within" (Gopinath 2005: 14). I have questioned the idea of coming out as a matter of individual choice, instead highlighting the role of the collective in negotiations of sexual identity (Decena 2008; Stella 2012; Peumans 2014). I also distinguished three dimensions through which the visibility paradigm could be challenged: (1) by negotiating contextually embedded expectations of visibility/coming out; (2) by illuminating the overlaps and fluid borders between visibility and invisibility; and (3) by providing an understanding of the family, the queer community, and the nation as multifaceted sites of struggle. My fieldwork data illuminates that non-heterosexual migrant women in this context primarily do not subscribe to a visibility/invisibility dichotomy, or a "Western" visibility paradigm. As these women were involved in different negotiations around the degree to which their romantic relationships should be a point of discussion in relation to their families and to the queer community, their positionings in relation to in/visibility differed. However, on a general level, their positionings appear as simultaneously in and out of the closet, or neither in nor out. These variegated dynamics, I suggest, highlight the importance of paying attention to context-specific and intersecting forms of power on multiple scales, as these women were embedded in broader ideological structures of homotolerance, Islamophobia, and homophobia, paradoxically making them at once hypervisible and invisible. Further, the racialized, sexualized and gendered boundaries that regulated access to belonging were challenged by the small space of the community in the organizations, constructing livable spaces through affective ties, emerging from collective frameworks of everyday experience. Finally, these dynamics illuminate the need to challenge the emphasis on visibility in much queer scholarship and activism, making room for more nuanced understandings of a variety of non-heterosexual identities, practices, and relationships as forms of queer livability beyond dominant images of out and proud visibilities.

Acknowledgments

I am indebted to my research participants, who shared invaluable experiences and knowledges around non-heterosexual lives and liveabilities. I would also like to thank the participants in the Transnational Solidarities workshop at the University of Gothenburg in May 2018, for constructive feedback. I am grateful for the support of guest editor Eithne Luibhéid and for the insightful feedback from the three anonymous peer review readers.

Funding

This article was written within the project "Spaces of Resistance: A Study of Gender and Sexualities in Times of Transformation," supported by the Knut and Alice Wallenberg Foundation under reference number 2015.0180.

References

Abu-Lughod, Lila (1990) "The Romance of Resistance: Tracing Transformations of Power through Bedouin Women," *American Anthropological Association*, 17:1, 41–55.

Akin, Deniz (2017) "Queer Asylum Seekers: Translating Sexuality in Norway," *Journal of Ethnic and Migration Studies*, 43:3, 458–474.

Akin, Deniz (2019) "The 'Ungrateful' Queer Refugee," presentation workshop 2, *Transforming Identities: Challenging Nordic Exceptionalisms*, University of Gothenburg, May 8–10.

Alinia, Minoo (2011) "Gender Equal Racism and Barbarian Immigrants: 'Honor violoence, and the Politics of Difference.'" In *In Topographies of Violence*, edited by Carina Listerborn, Irene Molina, and Diana Mulinari, 287–328. Stockholm, Sweden: Atlas.

Avrahami, Dina (2007) *We are not Dancing on the Table*. Stockholm, Sweden: Pickabook Förlag.

Biswas, Ranjita, Niharika Banerjea, Rukmini Banerjee, Sumita B. with special inputs from Katherine Browne, Nick McGlynn, and Leela Bakshi (2016) Understanding Liveability/ies: A Report of Making Liveable Lives: Rethinking Social Exclusion: A Transnational Activist-Academic Research Project. Kolkata, India: Sappho for Equality.

Bolsø, Agnes (2008) "Mission Accomplished?" *Trikster*, 1, 1–11.

Boym, Svetlana (1998) "On Diasporic Intimacy: Ilya Kabakov's Installations and Immigrant Homes," *Critical Inquiry*, 24, 498–524.

Browne, Kath, Niharika Banerjea, Nick McGlynn, Sumita B., Leela Bakshi, Rukmini Banerjee, and Ranjita Biswas (2017) "Towards Transnational Feminist Queer Methodologies," *Gender, Place and Culture: A Journal of Feminist Geography*, 24:10, 1376–397.

Butler, Judith (2004) *Undoing Gender*. New York, NY: Routledge.

Dahl, Ulrika (2009) "Queer in the Nordic Region: Telling Queer (Feminist) Stories." In *Queer in Europe*, edited by Lisa Downing and Robert Gillett, 143–158. London, England: Ashgate.

Decena, Carlos Ulises (2008) "Tacit Subjects," *GLQ: A Journal of Lesbian and Gay Studies*, 14:2–3, 339–359.

El-Tayeb, Fatima (2012) *European Others*. Minneapolis: University of Minnesota Press.

Esack, Farid and Nadeem Mahomed (2011) "Sexual Diversity, Islamic Jurisprudence and Sociality," *Journal of Gender and Religion*, 17:2, 41–57.

Göle, Nilüfer (2011) "The Public Visibility of Islam and European Politics of Resentment: The Minarets-Mosques Debate," *Philosophy and Social Criticism*, 37:4, 383–392.

Gopinath, Gayatri (2005) *Impossible Desires: Queer Diasporas and South Asian Public Cultures*. Durham, NC: Duke University Press.

Gopinath, Gayatri (2018) *Unruly Visions: The Aesthetic Practices of Queer Diaspora*. Durham, NC: Duke University Press.

Keskinen, Suvi, Sari Irni, Diana Mulinari, and Salla Tuori (eds.) (2009) *Complying with Colonialism*. London, England: Ashgate.

Leinonen Johanna and Mari Toivanen (2014) "Researching In/Visibility in the Nordic Context: Theoretical and Empirical Views," *Nordic Journal of Migration Research*, 4:4, 161–167.

Liinason, Mia (2018a) *Equality Struggles: Women's Movements, Neoliberal Markets and State Political Agendas in Scandinavia*. London, England: Routledge.

Liinason, Mia (2018b) "Borders and Belongings in Nordic Feminisms and Beyond," *Gender, Place and Culture: A Journal of Feminist Geography*, 25:7, 1041–1056.

Loftsdóttir, Kristín and Lars Jensen (eds.) (2016) *Whiteness and Postcolonialism in the Nordic Region*. London, England: Taylor and Francis.

Luibhéid, Eithne (2014) "Afterword: Troubling Identities and Identifications," *Sexualities*, 17:8, 1035–1040.

Manalansan IV, Martin F. (1997) "In the Shadows of Stonewall: Examining Gay Transnational Politics and the Diasporic Dilemma." In *The Politics of Culture in the Shadow of Capital*, edited by Lisa Lowe and David Lloyd, 485–505. Durham, NC: Duke University Press.

McNevin, Anne (2009) "Contesting Citizenship: Irregular Migrants and Strategic Possibilities for Political Belonging," *New Political Science*, 31:2, 163–181.

Mulinari, Diana, Suvi Keskinen, Sari Irni, and Salla Tuori (2009) "Introduction: Postcolonialism and the Nordic Models of Welfare and Gender." In *Complying with Colonialism*, edited by Diana Mulinari, Suvi Keskinen, Sari Irni, and Salla Tuori, 16–46. London, England: Ashgate.

Neufeld, Masha (2018) "On the Periphery of the Magical Closets—(Self) Representations and (Non) Visibility of Lesbians in Russia," presentation *Transnational Solidarities: Gender and Sexualities beyond Geopolitics*, University of Gothenburg, May 23–24.

Peumans, Wim (2014) "Queer Muslim Migrants in Belgium: A Research Note on Same-Sex Sexualities," *Sexualities*, 17:5–6, 618–631.

Puar, Jasbir (2007) *Terrorist Assemblages*. Durham, NC: Duke University Press.

Sager, Maja (2018) "Struggles around Representation and In/Visibility in Everyday Migrant Irregularity in Sweden," *Nordic Journal of Migration Research*, 8:3, 175–182.

Shakhsari, Sima (2014) "The Queer Time of Death: Temporality, Geopolitics, and Refugee rRghts," *Sexualities*, 17:8, 998–1015.

Siraj, Asifa (2011) "Isolated, Invisible, and in the Closet: The Life Story of a Scottish Muslim Lesbian," *Journal of Lesbian Studies*, 15:1, 99–121.

Spivak, Gayatri Chakravorty (2004) "Righting Wrongs," *The South Atlantic Quarterly*, 103: 2–3, 523–581.

Stella, Francesca (2012) "The Politics of In/Visibility: Carving Out Queer Space in Ul'yanovsk," *Europe-Asia Studies*, 64:10, 1822–1846.

Stella, Franscesca (2015) *Lesbian Lives in Soviet and Post-Soviet Russia: Post/Socialism and Gendered Sexualities*. Houndmills, Basingstoke, Hampshire: Palgrave Macmillan.

Strømsvik, Ida Dalslåen (2017) *Embodying Intersecting Selves*. Oslo, Norway: University of Oslo.

White, Melissa Autumn (2013) "Ambivalent Homonationalisms," *Interventions*, 15:1, 37–54.

Coming out and going abroad: The *chuguo* mobility of queer women in China

Lucetta Y. L. Kam

ABSTRACT
This article is part of a research project that explores the movement of queer women (lesbian, bisexual, transgender, and queer identified) from China to Australia and other Western countries. The research is based on participant observation and interviews that were conducted in selected cities in China and Australia. This article centers on queer women's narratives and experiences of going abroad, *chuguo*. Economic and social transformations in China have given rise to a new class of mobile urbanites. Going abroad has become a preferred life plan for young elites and the single child generation from urban, middle-class family backgrounds. The author looks at how mobility, sexuality, and gender non-conformity are intertwined in queer women's crafting of their life aspirations, and how the normative aspiration of *chuguo* in contemporary China enables (and disables) new ways of living and being. Building on the author's previous theorization of the "politics of public correctness," it is argued that transnational mobility has become a new homonormative value, which interplays with the neoliberal desire to be a mobile cosmopolitan subject in post-socialist China.

Introduction

I met Rebecca and Becky[1] in 2006 when I was conducting fieldwork for my research project about queer women (*lalas*[2]) in Shanghai. They were both in their mid-twenties, born and grew up in Shanghai, and had been together for two years at that time. Rebecca was an IT professional and Becky was a lecturer. They met through *lala* friends they knew from the Internet. Early to mid-2000 was the formative period of the local *lala* community in Shanghai and in China generally. Young urban professional women like Rebecca and Becky were taking advantage of the availability of the Internet and the emergence of commercial and community spaces for lesbian and gay people in cities. The biggest difficulty that Rebecca and Becky faced at that time was the pressure to marry and how to negotiate with their families about their sexuality. Since they could not find other ways to be together and resist marriage pressure from their families, they planned to go abroad. Over the next decade, I kept in touch with them throughout their process of applying for migration to and finally settling down in Australia. Sexuality and migration were two themes that tremendously transformed this couple's life trajectory. Their story demonstrates an emerging form of queer life that becomes available to certain groups of people in and from China. Through transnational mobility and migration, queer women from China are able to imagine and realize a life that can partially relieve them from the heteronormative demands they experience at home. The use of mobility capital, defined by Kaufmann et al. (2004) as a form of capital that can be exchanged for other types of capital, becomes an increasingly popular way for queer women to negotiate their gender and sexual non-normativity with their family and obtain recognition and protection for their same-sex relationship. For some of them, the process and possibility of living as a queer person are realized through transnational mobility.

This article is part of a research project[3] about the mobility of queer women from China, which is an extension of my last ethnographic study about queer women (*lalas*) in Shanghai (conducted during 2005–2011). Through this study, I hope to offer new insights into the lives of queer women from China in overseas countries and, more importantly, the emergent forms of queer self, life, aspirations, and mobility of a new generation of transnationally mobile queer women in China. The current literature on queer migration has limited discussion of queer women from China in Australia. The official website of the Australian Bureau of Statistics for 2016 shows that China-born residents are the third biggest group in the country, just after UK- and New Zealand-born populations, and the biggest Asia-born population group in Australia.[4] The most common reason my informants gave for choosing Australia as a destination is its comparatively friendly migration policies in terms of language requirements, professional qualifications, and length of application period. For prospective students, the attractions include the relatively less competitive entry requirements for universities in Australia and geographical proximity to China. Given the popularity of Australia as a destination for queer women from China for transnational migration and study, and its growing Chinese population, it is hoped that this research project can contribute to the existing literature on queer migration and transnational Chinese studies in two ways. First, the project enhances understanding of this emerging but understudied group of queer women against a larger picture of transnational queer mobility and migration; and second, it explores the intersection of sexuality, gender non-conformity, and transnational mobility among Chinese people, with a focus on the experiences of queer women. In this article, I will share stories of how mobility and sexuality are intertwined in queer women's stories of transnational movement and how their motivations and aspirations are informed by homonormative values. Primarily built on my earlier discussion of the politics of public correctness (Kam 2013), I argue that the practice of going abroad (*chuguo*) has to be understood in the context of the pursuit of a cosmopolitan self in post-socialist China, and in the context of the politics of public correctness that finds a new avenue of expression in the socially desirable act of *chuguo*. Transnational mobility has contributed to new homonormative values concerning how to become a good queer person in cosmopolitan and post-socialist China.

In the sections that follow, I first explain my methodology and describe informants' backgrounds. Next, I offer a brief discussion of how I situate my informants within the current trend of queer mobility and migration. The following section explains the social context of *chuguo* mobility in contemporary China. In the last section, I explore queer women's motivations and aspirations for transnational mobility, arguing that mobility has become a new homonormative value and expression of the politics of public correctness.

Methodology and informants

I started this project about mobile Chinese queer women in 2015. I conducted most of the interviews and participant observation (in Melbourne) during 2016–2018. Excluding the women I interviewed for a pilot study in 2015, I conducted twenty-eight interviews from 2016 to 2018 in Australia and China. Informants include international Chinese students (who studied in Australia and other countries, such as the United States and the United Kingdom), working holiday goers, recently arrived immigrants in Australia, transcontinental commuters between China and Australia, and young urban women in China who are planning to go abroad. Most of the informants in Australia lived in Melbourne and a few in Sydney, Cairns, Brisbane, and Adelaide. Informants in China lived in Beijing, Shanghai, Shenzhen, and Hong Kong.[5] Interviews were semi-structured, in-depth, face-to-face, audio-recorded, and a few were conducted via email. Email interviews were conducted with informants who resided outside Melbourne, with those in Melbourne I could not meet in person, and with those in China who I could not visit due to time and funding restrictions. Most interviews were conducted individually, while a few were conducted with the couple together. Most interviews were conducted in Mandarin, with only one in English upon the request of the informant.

I divided my informants into the following four groups: (1) the major group: international students and recently arrived immigrants in Australia from China; (2) those who travel regularly between Australia and China; (3) those in China who are planning to go abroad; and (4) those who have returned to China from overseas countries (not limited to Australia).

I used the umbrella term "queer" to identify my informants in this study. Most of them identified themselves as lesbian. Some of them identified as bisexual and a few wrote "fluid," "pansexual," or "not yet decided" in the pre-interview information questionnaire. For gender identification, most of them identified as "female," while a few specified their gender/sexual role in lesbian relationship, such as "H" ("half," which means *lalas* with a more androgynous gender style and a sexual preference that is not restricted to T or P), "P" ("*po*," feminine *lala*) or "passive T" (*shou* T, in which T means masculine *lala*). One informant identified herself as "queer" for gender and another one wrote "sometimes male sometimes female." Their ages ranged from twenty-one to forty-seven, with the majority in their late twenties to thirties. Most of them were the single child in their family. Seven of them have been or were in a heterosexual marriage at the time of the interview. Among this group, four were divorced, two were in a cooperative marriage (a consensual marriage between a gay man and a lesbian woman), and one was in a five-year heterosexual marriage. The two divorced informants each have a child from their previous marriage. Nine informants were in an officially registered same-sex marriage or de facto same-sex partnership. All had or were about to have a bachelor's degree or higher. For those who were working in Australia at the time of the interview, their occupations included early childhood teacher, IT professional, self-employed designer, artist, photographer, social worker, chef, and owner of a consultancy firm and travel agency. A few of them were studying in undergraduate or master's programs. Their length of stay in Australia ranged from one to thirteen years. Most of them had obtained permanent residency, while a few were still applying for it and a few were already citizens at the time of the interview. They initially entered Australia on a student, skilled migration, dependent (through registered same-sex partnership or marriage in Australia or other countries), working holiday, or family connection visa. Among the younger informants in my study, many came from middle-class families with parents who were managers of state-owned enterprises, junior to middle-range state officials, or professionals such as accountant, teacher, designer, engineer, or business owner.

Queerness and transnational mobility

New forms of intimate relationships, kinship and family formed by transnational or transcontinental movement, whether queer or straight, have been documented in detail and analyzed by ethnographers, cultural theorists, and sociologists (Binnie 2004; Cheng 2010; Cruz-Malave and Manalansan 2002; Giddens 1992; Hull 2006; Kong 2011; Luibheid 2002, 2008; Martin 2014, 2017; Patton and Sanchez-Eppler 2000; Plummer 2003). The *GLQ* issue of *Queer/Migration* was one of the first efforts to explore "the multiple conjunctions between sexuality and migration" in scholarship (Luibheid 2008, 169). In that issue, Audrey Yue documents the development of queer migration to Australia before the official recognition of same-sex marriage, especially exploring how sexual law and policy reforms contributed to "the emergence of Australian queer modernity" (Yue 2008, 239) against the backdrop of the promotion of multiculturalism. Yue shows how early same-sex migration policies reinforced heteronormative values such as good moral conduct of the family and relationships. Her discussion sheds light on how some of my informants actively planned their same-sex relationship and future based on the legal models that are currently available in countries where same-sex couples are eligible to enter and stay. With the recognition of same-sex relationships, partnerships, and marriages in migration policies in many countries, and the globalization of queer culture through the circulation of ideas, images, media texts, commodities and business models, more and more resources are available for queer people to imagine or plan for a life in a place they think will be better. The migration policies and models of homonormative intimacy in the host society and the new homonormative values of a good queer person in post-socialist China (further explained later in the article) work together to inform queer women's motivations and aspirations for transnational mobility. Travis Kong's ethnography of Chinese gay men's transnational mobility demonstrates the various influences queer globalization has exerted on mobile gay men in their search to become sexual citizens in different localities (Kong 2011). Their stories were shaped by the politics of race, sexuality, class, and gender in Hong Kong, China, and London in the contexts of post-colonialism and globalization. In my project, I position my informants as a significant group of participants in contemporary global queer migration and mobility. Their transnational mobility is an integral part of this global trend. I intend to document and collect those yet-to-be-told stories of queer women from China who are participating in the global movement of queer migration and in the process of developing new forms of queer subjectivity and living inside and outside China.

The social context of *chuguo* mobility

Before the market reform in 1979, when geographical and social mobility were unlikely to be achieved through individual effort, the act of *chuguo* or international travel was a highly privileged one. It signified social, political, and economic privilege in socialist China. Since the reform era, the prestige or myth of *chuguo* continued, while economic and social transformations have given rise to a new class of mobile urbanites. Going abroad has become a preferred life plan for young elites and the single child generation from urban, middle-class family backgrounds. To have the resources and ability to plan a life abroad constitutes a form of upward social mobility.

Chuguo points to a bright future, one that is very much desired by today's young people and their parents. Geographical mobility can lead to social mobility, and social mobility is expressed through geographical mobility. Mobility becomes a quality one strives to acquire in order to pursue a good or successful life. A mobile self with "portable personhood" (Elliott and Urry 2010, 3) is highly desired by the younger generation of urban Chinese women and often actively supported by their parents. The parents of my informants have witnessed the transition of China into a market economy since the 1980s and the general longing to become a new, cosmopolitan Chinese subject. Lisa Rofel extensively discusses how the pursuit of a "global self" (Rofel 2007) that embraces cosmopolitanism and strives to transcend the local impacted the young urban women in China in the 1990s. The pursuit of a "global self has not only continued into the new millennium but also extended to become a project that is aspired by young women, and men, from a wide range of social classes and economic backgrounds in China (De Kloet and Fung 2017). In present-day China, the aspiration to become "desirable, globalized subjects" (Rofel 2007, 126) is not only expressed through the practices of consumption, but is fulfilled in most cases by the act of going abroad. Now people have more options to achieve this goal. The tourism boom in China and the exploding number of Chinese tourists abroad demonstrate people's desire to travel. Through travel or transnational mobility, one comes closer to embracing that cosmopolitan global self. This desire is echoed in many of my informants' narratives of the reasons for their transnational mobility. The urge to experience freedom, a new life, a different kind of life, a life that is away from the pressure (such as exams, family) and repressive political atmosphere in China are common reasons for going abroad. The yearning for a global self is also expressed through their aspirations to live freely as a queer person; in some cases, as a recognized same-sex couple or family.

Most queer women in this research project were born in the 1990s. They grew up at a time when China, especially in urban areas, started to have more available resources and public discussion of homosexuality and alternative genders. Their stories of coming to terms with their own sexuality and gender identification, and coming out to family, are different from the stories I heard ten years earlier. Pressure to marry remains a major difficulty for many queer women in their twenties. But it is noticeable that there are more discourses and resources available for them to resist or negotiate these heteronormative demands. One controversial "solution" involves cooperative marriage. Going abroad is another popular option for queer women with mobility capital who seek to avoid marriage, even though it is not a guaranteed solution. These women belong to an emergent urban mobile population in post-socialist China. Mobility forms a significant part of their everyday life and long-term life course planning. The women in my study belonged to this group of people.

Mobility as a new normative value

Sexuality and gender-nonconformity have played a role in my informants' stories of mobility. The normative aspiration for *chuguo* in contemporary China directs queer women to imagine new life possibilities outside China. In post-socialist China, *chuguo* becomes a new normative demand for being a good *tongzhi* (a Mandarin Chinese term that literally means "comrades," which has been used as a local identity for the LGBTQI+ communities in China since the term was first introduced in Hong Kong and Taiwan in the late 1980s). In my earlier project about Shanghai *lalas,* I introduced the term "politics of public correctness" to refer to a general belief or normative demand for being a publicly correct person before one comes out to live as a *tongzhi* (Kam 2013). To many of the informants in that earlier project, being a publicly correct person meant being "a law-abiding citizen, an economically productive member of society, an obedient daughter and a 'model' homosexual (that is, one who fits into the homonormative imagination of 'healthy' and 'sunny' representations)" (Kam 2013, 90). The politics of normalization dominated activist rhetoric in the first decade of 2000 in China. "Healthy" (*jiankang*) and "sunny" (*yangguang*) were two keywords that frequently appeared in the publications and slogans in the *tongzhi* community at that time, challenging images of *tongzhi* as pathetic, pathological, or living in the dark. Thus, the politics of public correctness developed at a time when the anti-stigmatization of homosexuality took priority over other demands such as diversity, equal rights, and a queer understanding of gender and sexuality within the *tongzhi* community. When transnational mobility or *chuguo* increasingly became a norm for the younger urban population and professional class in China, mobility became incorporated into the politics of public correctness for queer subjects. Being queer and mobile adds up to a new model of how to be a good and respectful *tongzhi* in China.

In the next section, I discuss informants' motivations and aspirations for transnational mobility, showing that mobility has become a new homonormative desire and a new expression of the politics of public correctness. I explore queer women's motivation for transnational mobility and the role of sexuality in the process; their experience of transnational mobility and how it informs their sexuality and intimate lives; and how they negotiate sexuality before and after leaving.

Motivations and aspirations

For queer women I interviewed, the typical plan of *chuguo* involves getting high school, university, or postgraduate education in Australia, sometimes with financial help from their parents. Some of them stayed after graduation to work and apply for permanent residency (PR). A few arrived in Australia through skilled migration.

Queer Chinese women's decision to go abroad is shaped by the broader social understanding of *chuguo*, and young people's use of *chuguo* to escape highly competitive university entry examinations or look for more cultural exposure outside China. For some queer women, leaving home and their immediate social circles is also an exit available to escape heteronormative demands, such as gender conformity and marriage.

The word "*yayi*" in Mandarin, which can be translated into "stressful and repressed," occurred frequently in many informants' narrative of early life experience in China as a teenager or young woman. The experience of their same-sex attraction being discovered by parents and school during their early years in China, and the unfriendly and stressful atmosphere they felt at home and school, are two themes that appeared in many of their memories of life in China. Twenty-nine-year-old Linda's story shows how these experiences pushed her to leave China for Australia to study after she finished high school.

Linda was born and grew up in north China. She developed a romantic relationship with her female high school classmate. Her same-sex first love was discovered and brutally intervened into by teachers. After the school informed her parents, they took her to seek medical help. Later, she was forced to change schools and not allowed to see her girlfriend again. She started to realize that it would be impossible for her to have same-sex relationships if she stayed in China and with her parents. She suggested to her parents that she wanted to study abroad, which they fully supported. So, soon after she finished high school, she left China for Melbourne to start undergraduate study. At the time of our interview, she has been living in Melbourne for about ten years. Even through transnational mobility, she was not able to fully escape marriage pressure, especially when she reached the marriage age. To deal with her parents' expectation, she entered into a cooperative marriage with an Australian partner.

For informants like Linda, who came out before they left China, transnational mobility is an active choice they make to live away from their parents and normative social demands in China. Aspirations to be free from parental control while avoiding direct confrontation are common for informants across age groups. Even queer women who have passed the age of marriage pressure want to create physical and emotional distance from their parents. Physical distance offers a protection to queer women who are not accepted by their family in China. Eligibility to study or work abroad allows them to fulfill these goals while also becoming desirable, cosmopolitan, and culturally competent subjects. In the logic of the politics of public correctness, queer women's mobility capital can, to some extent, "compensate" for their non-normative sexuality and failure to lead a heteronormative life.

Informants in this study include women in their late thirties to mid-forties who were professionally and economically well-established in China. Transnational migration brings this group of Chinese queer women legal protection for their assets and relationships, but they have to give up the more comfortable life they used to enjoy in China. Many leave behind well-established social and business networks, family support, and the class privileges they used to enjoy. For example, Emma and her same-sex partner landed in Australia together as a couple. They were in their forties and both had been in heterosexual marriages. Emma's partner had a young child who joined them in Australia in their second year there. Before migration, Emma and her partner both had stable careers in their respective professions. Their major reason for leaving China was to achieve full recognition of their same-sex relationship and family. In China, they were unable to live openly as same-sex parents and family. They were invisible to other people and did not have a place in state policies.

> Emma: "In fact we lived a very happy life [in China]. It's quite good. But an important reason [for going abroad] is that there's no way for us to share our joy. Our family life… a marriage between a man and a woman and a marriage between two women are actually the same. Then when other people ask me how come you're still single, [then you know] they still see you as a single person. So we can't find a way to share our personal life and to tell them it's really happy. […] Our relationship does not exist in the eye of the Chinese government… At least at the policy level, we're entirely invisible. We don't have that recognition."

Emma mentioned aspiring to "freedom," "self-identification," "sense of belonging," and "feeling secure" through transnational migration. She envisioned a future of living as a socially and legally recognized same-sex couple and family in Australia, even though she and her partner have to renegotiate their financial status and economic well-being in the new society.

The yearning for recognition is echoed by another couple who decided to migrate to Sydney from Beijing. Carrie and Jackie ran a prosperous business in Beijing before they applied for skilled migration to Australia. During their ten-year relationship, they had come out to their immediate families and friends in China, but could not live openly as a same-sex couple in their business community or have legal recognition and protection as a couple. By law, they were not even allowed to open a joint bank account and co-own property, since the law does not allow same-sex couples any legal status in financial, medical, and social welfare arrangements.

> Carrie: "At that place [Australia], you can be in broad daylight. Let me give you an example. The medical card we have in Australia, we share the same card, which means our card has both of our names on it. Everything of us is recognized."

Their aspiration for transnational mobility and foreign passports echoes other transnational Chinese subjects who are actively seeking "flexible citizenship" (Ong 1999), while at the same time working to preserve their privileged status in China as much as possible. They aspire to enjoy protection and recognition as queer people overseas, while still keeping their established business connection and privileged status in China. Their new home and life in Sydney are planned as an extension of their established life in China. They travel frequently between China and Australia to maintain the two homes and their business in China.

For some informants, sexuality or gender non-conformity was not initially their reason for transnational mobility. But when they reached marital age, usually from the early twenties to late twenties, pressure pushed them to think about remaining abroad. Joey (twenty-nine years old) was a kindergarten teacher who had lived in Melbourne for nearly ten years. She grew up in a relatively liberal family and came out to them before leaving China. Sexuality was not a significant factor in her initial decision to leave. But heterosexual gender norms and the social expectation that one should lead a heteronormative life in her hometown were concerns that she always mentioned in her interview, which kept her from returning to China as she grew older.

> Joey: "You can do what you want to do here [Melbourne]. If I go back... almost all my exes are married with kids! [...] People here also complain about their life, but I think I can still make a change. They [female friends in hometown] just think it's impossible. [...] Turning thirty is a new beginning. In China it's like... getting settled down is more important. Fewer people will try to get what they want. Perhaps there's more to lose if they do. They think they can't live a precarious life. Here, I can just work hard to get what I want. In China, if you want anything, you got to first try very hard to change other people's values before you do anything. That's more tiring...."

Joey's view on China is quite typical among informants who had left for a relatively longer period of time, such as over ten years. As Fran Martin's

(2014, 2017) study of female international students in Australia shows, the pursuit of an autonomous self by young women in their twenties through transnational mobility cannot save them from the heteronormative gender demands that are imposed on them as they get older. For queer women like Joey, even though transnational mobility was not initially related to sexuality, heteronormative pressure increased as they grew older or finished study, prompting many to stay in Australia after graduation. Thus, Kris, in her early forties, started to plan for migration when she was in her late twenties. A lesbian friend who had migrated to Australia inspired her to go abroad. She had a stable job and a well-off life in her hometown. The pressure of marriage prompted her to leave China. She has never come out to her parents, who lived in the same town and persistently pressured Kris to get married. The experience of her lesbian friend living in Australia with her same-sex partner encouraged Kris to apply for skilled migration. In her mid-thirties, she moved to Melbourne. When I met Kris in Melbourne, she was struggling with her new business and life in a foreign country as a new immigrant.

To queer people with mobility capital, transnational mobility constitutes one of the emerging aspects of politics of public correctness. It is a practice that enables them to live away from family pressures and social constraints in China and exhibit qualities of a desirable mobile Chinese subject. Whether the new life abroad is as good as one imagines, the practice of *chuguo* is becoming a possible and popular way out for queer people with mobility capital in China. But it is still a privileged move.

Conclusion

This article highlights the relationship between transnational mobility and sexuality and how queer self and life are realized, shaped, and negotiated through the mobility of *chuguo*. I discuss how transnational mobility has become a new expression of the politics of public correctness for queer women in China to negotiate heteronormative demands. Mobility forms a core quality of the modern Chinese subject and *chuguo* has become a normative desire. To my informants, the more supportive and friendly social environment that they expect in Western countries towards queer people is a major attraction to imagine and plan for a life abroad. The possibility of living away from heteronormative demands, and the recognition of same-sex relationship and family, are enabled by the option of *chuguo*. The motivation and aspiration of queer women to go abroad include those normative, non-sexuality-related desires that are shared by other Chinese people in transnational mobility and migration and, at the same time, sexuality- and gender-specific causes have pushed them to imagine a life outside China. To live away from the stressful social and political environment in China and their immediate family, to have legal protection and recognition of their same-sex relationship, to live freely as a queer person, to avoid the heteronormative demands imposed on women, are aspirations that are shared by many informants for transnational mobility.

When I listen to those stories of queer women from China, it is not hard to find that some stories would easily fit into a homonormative framework—such as the celebration of material achievements, the pursuit of a "normal" life that includes a stable monogamous relationship, a self-reliant lifestyle, and sometimes the possibility of having children. There were times I was "disappointed" by those stories, because they sounded so similar to those I heard more than a decade ago in China when the *tongzhi* community was at its formative period and an exclusive same-sex relationship was still a lifestyle experiment. I was looking for something "different" or even "radical" in queer women's stories. But after I met more queer women in Australia and China and listened to their stories of mobility, I found that it might be misguided to look for stories that are "different." Going abroad is a new strategy for queer women in China to avoid direct confrontation with family or being seen as a social outcast and, at the same time, a means to live as a queer person. Therefore, the practice of *chuguo* has to be understood as a new expression of the politics of public correctness. If cooperative marriage appropriates the surface order of a heterosexual marriage, then going abroad fulfills the normative desire of being a global and cosmopolitan Chinese subject in post-socialist China. Mobility becomes a new and essential part of the politics of public correctness and a new survival strategy for some privileged queer people to avoid or delay the heteronormative demands that are imposed on them. The stories of queer mobile Chinese women demonstrate how heteronormative demands and neoliberal values in post-socialist China, such as the emphasis on mobility capital, cosmopolitanism, and global experiences, interplay with emergent models of homonormativity, such as same-sex marriage and rainbow parenthood, urban middle-class *tongzhi*, and the global and mobile Chinese queer. Together, they form new routes of queer mobility and life trajectories.

Notes

1. Informants' names used in this article are all pseudonyms. Their personal information is also altered to protect their identity.
2. Most women in my study identify themselves by the local term "*lala*," which means lesbian, bisexual, and queer (*ku'er* in Mandarin Chinese) women. I use "*lala*" when I intend to highlight the local specificity or cite directly from interviews. I use "queer" to refer to women with non-heterosexual identifications, as an umbrella term for women with non-heterosexual gender and sexual identifications, and when I refer to

established academic terms such as "queer mobility and migration." I use the two terms interchangeably with the recognition that they are not entirely equivalent in the context of China. I also use "*tongzhi*" in this article to refer to the wider LGBTQI+ communities in China. I use "mobility" to refer to a broad range of geographical movements for recreation, education, or employment, and "migration" to refer to long-term settlement in the host society.

3. The research project was funded by the General Research Fund (2016–18) offered by the University Grants Committee in Hong Kong.
4. Australian Bureau of Statistics (Information retrieved on May 10, 2019): http://www.abs.gov.au/AUSSTATS/abs@.nsf/mf/3412.0
5. Permanent residents in Hong Kong were not included in this study. All informants were either citizens of the People's Republic of China (PRC) or originally came from the PRC at the time of the interview. One informant was interviewed in Hong Kong because she was working in Hong Kong at the time of the interview.

Acknowledgments

This article has traveled through a long journey to arrive at this version. The author would like to sincerely thank the editor for the detailed reading and very helpful feedback on the earlier drafts. This article has also benefitted from the advice of Fran Martin, Audrey Yue, John Erni, and many who listened to my presentations at conferences. The author is also grateful to Eleanor Cheung, Yiu Fai Chow, and Daisy Tam for their feedback and encouragement throughout the revision process. Lastly, the author thanks all informants in this project for sharing with me their intimate stories.

References

Binnie, Jon. 2004. *The Globalization of Sexuality*. London, England: Sage Publications.
Cheng, Sealing. 2010. *On the Move for Love: Migrant Entertainers and the U.S. Military in South Korea*. Philadelphia, PA: University of Pennsylvania Press.
Cruz-Malave, Arnaldo and Martin F. Manalansan IV, eds. 2002. *Queer Globalizations: Citizenship and the Afterlife of Colonialism*. New York, NY: New York University Press.
De Kloet, Jeroen and Anthony Fung. 2017. *Youth Cultures in China*. Cambridge, England: Polity Press.
Elliott, Anthony and John Urry. 2010. *Mobile Lives*. London, England: Routledge.
Giddens, Anthony. 1992. *The Transformation of Intimacy: Sexuality, Love, and Eroticism in Modern Societies*. Cambridge, England: Polity Press.

Hull, Kathleen E. 2006. *Same-Sex Marriage: The Cultural Politics of Love and Law*. Cambridge, England: Cambridge University Press.

Kam, Yip Lo Lucetta. 2013. *Shanghai Lalas: Female Tongzhi Communities and Politics in Urban China*. Hong Kong: Hong Kong University Press.

Kaufmann, Vincent, Manfred Max Bergman, and Dominique Joye. 2004. "Motility: Mobility as Capital." *International Journal of Urban and Regional Research*, Volume 28, No. 4, pp. 745–756.

Kong, Travis S. K. 2011. *Chinese Male Homosexualities: Memba, Tongzhi and Golden Boy*. London, England: Routledge.

Luibheid, Eithne. 2002. *Entry Denied: Controlling Sexuality at the Border*. Minneapolis, MN: University of Minnesota Press.

Luibheid, Eithne. 2008. "Queer/Migration." *GLQ: A Journal of Lesbian and Gay Studies*, Volume 14, No. 203.

Martin, Fran. 2014. "The Gender of Mobility: Chinese Women Students' Self-Making through Transnational Education." *Intersections: Gender and Sexuality in Asia and the Pacific*, Issue 35, July. http://intersections.anu.edu.au/issue35/martin.htm

Martin, Fran. 2017. "Mobile Self-Fashioning and Gendered Risk: Rethinking Chinese Students' Motivations for Overseas Education." *Globalization, Societies and Education*, Volume 15, pp. 706–720.

Ong, Aihwa. 1999. *Flexible Citizenship: The Cultural Logics of Transnationality*. Durham, NC: Duke University Press.

Patton, Cindy and Benigno Sanchez-Eppler, eds. 2000. *Queer Diasporas*. Durham, NC: Duke University Press.

Plummer, Ken. 2003. *Intimate Citizenship: Private Decisions and Public Dialogues*. Montreal, Canada: McGill-Queen's University Press.

Rofel, Lisa. 2007. *Desiring China: Experiments in Neoliberalism, Sexuality, and Public Culture*. Durham, NC: Duke University Press.

Yue, Audrey. 2008. "Same-Sex Migration in Australia: From Interdependency to Intimacy." *GLQ: A Journal of Lesbian and Gay Studies*, Volume 14, No. 2–3, pp. 239–262.

Lesbian refugees in transit: The making of authenticity and legitimacy in Turkey

Elif Sarı

> **ABSTRACT**
> Turkey is a "transit" country, where refugees spend many years waiting before they have a chance to be resettled to a third country. During this liminal period of waiting, refugees have to pursue and legitimize their asylum claims with various state and parastatal asylum infrastructures, such as the Turkish asylum authority, the UNHCR, third countries' embassies, and national, international, and diasporic NGOs and aid providers. This article examines how Iranian lesbian refugees navigate these legal, governmental, and humanitarian bodies that make disparate demands to evaluate the "authenticity" of their identities and the "legitimacy" of their claims. I argue that, during the period of waiting in Turkey, lesbian refugees learn to master specific forms of telling and performance demanded by states, NGOs, and communities in order to carve space for themselves in a system that systematically discredits their sexualities. By continually tailoring their narratives and performances to conform to certain "lesbian types" prioritized by these institutions, organizations, and communities, refugees not only make themselves "authentic," "deserving," and "legitimate" subjects *within* established tropes, but also transform how they imagine and embody their own and others' sexualities and genders.

Introduction

Rosha and I are sitting in my small studio apartment, browsing the files on Rosha's external hard disk to find "lesbian photos" of her. I try to refrain from asking too many curious questions about these images that span ten years and two countries. It is already 3 AM and we need to finish preparing her "case verification," demanded by a non-governmental organization (NGO) in Toronto that facilitates LGBTQI-identified refugees' resettlement to Canada through private sponsorship programs. Yet, at times, we find ourselves in the world of memories: her birthday party back in Iran, a weekend getaway to *Shomal* (North) with her best friend, "[who] is also lesbian," Rosha tells me, crossing the Iran-Turkey border by train with her then-girlfriend, working in cardboard and textile factories in Turkey. As much as I am intrigued by her stories, I still focus my attention on "lesbian details." Each time I see a photo of her hugging or kissing her ex-girlfriend, or a rainbow flag in the frame, I pause to drag that image to the case verification file. I cheer when I find a photo that captures them snuggling in bed. "I think it's obvious now that I am lesbian," Rosha says, laughing. When it comes to cutting down these images to a few selections, I suggest we maintain a variety of Rosha's haircuts and colors to reveal the *longitude* of her lesbian identity. I also suggest we keep a handful of the rare photos of Rosha smiling. "I see what you're doing," she says mockingly, "You want to trick them into believing that I am a *fun lesbian*."

This is not the first time Rosha has attempted to prove her lesbian identity. When I met her in 2017, she had already spent four years in Turkey waiting for resettlement to a third country that would be willing to accept her. During this time, she was asked to verify her sexual orientation on several occasions, in a series of formal interviews with the United Nations High Commissioner for Refugees (UNHCR) and the Turkish asylum authority, as well as in semi-formal meetings with Turkish humanitarian organizations and Iranian queer diaspora organizations. Although overlapping in their demands for Rosha to prove her lesbian identity, each of these institutions and organizations has their own understanding of what counts as lesbian and who should be included in this category. Thus, Rosha has had to perform lesbianness differently, over and over again, since arriving in Turkey. This was her first time doing this over email, however, and she was not sure about what a Canadian NGO might want to see in order to believe that Rosha is *really* lesbian. Assuming that, as a Ph.D. student at a U.S. university, I would have a better grasp of Western lesbian codes and NGO culture, she asked for my help.

Queer migration scholarship has extensively documented how asylum adjudicators and refugee aid organizations rely on what David Murray (2016a: 41) calls a "template of authenticity" to differentiate "fake" applicants from "authentic" or "real" queers, a template that is largely informed by Western stereotypes and upper-class, White, gay behavioral norms (Hinger 2010; Jenicek et al. 2009; Lewis 2010; Miller 2005; Morgan 2006; Rehaag 2009). Others have extended this discussion by problematizing the asylum system's reliance on a particular set of racialized, gendered, sexualized, and classed "social aesthetics" (Cabot 2014) in determining "deserving" refugees (Ticktin 2011) and "legitimate" forms of suffering and persecution (Shakhsari 2014; Ticktin 2011). These practices of eligibility require refugees to demonstrate their worthiness for asylum not only by conforming to universalizing categories of sexuality and gender (Luibhéid 2014), but also by demonstrating their capacity to integrate into certain lifestyles, moral and economic values, and homonationalist ideals of the host country (Luibhéid 2008; Murray 2016b; Puar 2007; White 2013).

The vast majority of these studies, however, have examined the challenges refugees face as they lodge their asylum claims in refugee-receiving countries. This limits asylum to a nation-state framework, on the one hand, and to a legal process—specifically the refugee status determination interview—on the other. This article examines asylum in Turkey, a "transit country" where refugees spend many years waiting before they have a chance to be resettled to a third country.[1] Indeed, as the tightening asylum policies of third countries like the United States and Canada have drastically curtailed the prospects for refugees' resettlement, people like Rosha have been stranded in Turkey with unpredictable legal status for an undetermined period of time. This liminal period of waiting also requires the skillful navigation of various state and parastatal asylum infrastructures. While they wait in Turkey, refugees have to constantly pursue and legitimize their asylum claims with the UNHCR, the Turkish immigration authorities, and the third countries' embassies and resettlement agencies (Biehl 2015). During a series of interviews conducted by these legal, humanitarian, and administrative bodies, they need to prove their gender identity and sexual orientation in order to establish their "membership in a particular group," and to give meticulous, emotive details about the violence they endured at home to demonstrate a "well-founded fear of persecution."

Furthermore, because the UNHCR and the Turkish state do not provide reliable financial and legal support during these periods of long and undetermined waiting, many LGBT refugees seek financial and legal aid from Iranian queer diaspora organizations based in Europe and North America. To become eligible for the services of these organizations, they undergo a series of in-person or online interviews, trying to prove their sexual orientation and/or gender identity and to justify their need for aid. Additionally, as the United States and Canada have been increasingly retrenching upon the prospect for government-sponsored resettlement, refugees have begun to reach out to Canadian queer NGOs, seeking private sponsorship as one of the few available resettlement paths.[2] Similar to their experiences with Iranian diaspora organizations, they are asked to verify their LGBTQI identity—this time not through interviews but, as Rosha's experience of case verification illustrates, by providing evidentiary documents such as photos, support letters, and medical reports.

I suggest that, in the context of asylum in Turkey, refugees face more than one "template of authenticity," as they navigate these private, public, and semi-public asylum apparatuses at national, international, and diasporic scales. While White/Western gay norms seem to dominate UNHCR's refugee status determination processes and third countries' resettlement processes, refugees also navigate local, national, and diasporic articulations of lesbianness during their encounters with Turkish immigration authorities, local aid providers, Iranian queer diaspora organizations, and other LGBT refugees. This article unpacks the repetitions and discontinuities among various "templates of authenticity" (Murray 2016a) and "social aesthetics" (Cabot 2014) to which refugees in Turkey are expected to conform. By attending to how refugees negotiate and reconcile these multiple expectations that sometimes conflict and sometimes overlap, it highlights the ways in which "the lesbian refugee" is articulated transnationally.[3]

Furthermore, in this liminal zone of waiting, articulations of "authenticity" and "deservingness" extend beyond the official refugee adjudication interviews and into more informal zones: lines in immigration offices while waiting for refugee identity cards and travel permits; community meetings organized by Iranian queer diaspora organizations; visits to Turkish charity organizations to seek financial aid; and emails soliciting private sponsorship sent to Canadian NGOs. In a different context, Eithne Luibhéid (2002: 79) depicts immigration checkpoints at the U.S.-Mexico border as "dense points where dominant institutions constructed (and individuals contested) the possible meanings of lesbian or gay identity and who should be included within these categories." Following her formulation, I approach these multiple sites, moments, and encounters—whether asylum interviews, travel permits, community meetings, or case verification emails—as critical sites where lesbianness is imagined, articulated, and policed in various ways based on disparate demands of different asylum agencies, NGOs, and aid providers.

The following sections explore how this transnational asylum system brings into being different categories of people, such as "fake lesbians," "full lesbians," or "golden case lesbians," as well as which "lesbian types" are prioritized over others and with what effects (Lewis 2010: 426). Further, keeping in mind that the process of categorization is hardly a unilateral exercise of power (Crenshaw 1989), I explore how refugees themselves negotiate, resist, and strategically utilize these categories to (re)claim their identities and facilitate their access to rights and protections. I argue that, during the period of waiting in Turkey, refugees learn to master specific forms of telling and performance demanded by states, NGOs, and communities in order to carve space for themselves in a system that systematically questions and discredits their sexualities. By doing so, they not only establish themselves as "authentic," "deserving," and "legitimate" subjects *within* established tropes, but also rearticulate and transform how they imagine and embody their own and others' sexualities and genders.

In this article, I utilize different sexual identity terminologies as they are articulated by asylum authorities, NGOs, and refugees. That is, when I write about asylum agencies and NGOs, I use their own terminology. The

UNHCR uses "LGBTI," Canadian NGOs I discuss in this article use "LGBTQI," and Iranian diaspora organizations use "queer" and "LGBT" to refer to the same group of people: those who lodge asylum claims on the grounds of sexual orientation and gender identity. These seemingly small differences have material consequences in refugees' lived lives, as their access to rights and protections hinges upon their ability to demonstrate that "they *are* those identities" (Luibhéid 2014: 1036). At other times, I use the term "LGBT" because that is how most of my interlocutors came to self-identify by the time they arrived in Turkey. Like "LGBT," "lesbian" is also a common self-identification, while I also heard people using other terms, such as "queer," "butch," "femme," "*verse*" (versatile), "*hamjansgara*" (same-sex orientation/homosexual), "having a girlfriend," and "*bachaye khodemun*" (our folk/one of us), to refer to themselves and others. More importantly, in line with my argument that identities are continually constructed and contested, made and remade, in this liminal time-space of waiting, I avoid universalizing and essentializing the term "lesbian," and instead aim to understand what it comes to signify in specific encounters between refugees, asylum adjudicators, aid providers, and Iranian and Canadian queer NGOs.

Methodology

I conducted twenty-three months of ethnographic research between 2015 and 2019 with Iranian LGBT refugees who lodged their asylum claims in Turkey, waiting for resettlement to a third country. My main field site was Denizli, a small town where the Turkish state relocates most LGBT refugees, though I also traveled to Kayseri, Eskisehir, Ankara, and Istanbul to meet other LGBT refugees. I spent the bulk of my fieldwork participating in refugees' everyday lives, sharing mundane and intimate practices of living together. I went to their homes, or they came to mine, we cooked together, watched films, played cards, drank Iranian homemade apple vodka (*araghe sib*), showed each other old photos, and talked for hours, sometimes until dawn. Life outside home in this small town was spatially and socially limited; we spent many days sitting in the same café, drinking black tea and smoking for hours, window shopped in the same mall almost every other day, and went to the only club in town every Saturday night.

The fact that I was out as a lesbian/queer woman in the field, was in the same age group as most of my interlocutors, and was always *paye* (a slang word they used to describe me as someone who is usually *in*, or *up for* a proposed plan) for most of the things they did, I became a fairly organic part of the community. My interlocutors often introduced me to other LGBTs as "*bachaye khodemun*" (our folk/one of us), a Farsi phrasing that refers to one's similitude with the rest of a group or community—in my case, referring to our shared daily engagements, but more so to our shared sexual identifications. In addition to our regular "hanging outs," I was present and deeply engaged in all communal events—weekly lesbian meetings, queer film screenings, picnics, self-care and sexual health seminars, and drama, storytelling, and dance workshops—organized by the UNHCR, national and international NGOs, and Iranian queer diaspora organizations.

I also conducted semi-structured interviews with more than sixty refugees. I learned as much from listening to them as I did from accompanying them to hospitals, immigration authorities, local NGOs, and charity organizations. As someone born and raised in Turkey, my language fluency and my ease at navigating legal, medical, and bureaucratic worlds made those "participant observation" visits more about "participation" than "observation." I made appointments, filed paperwork, translated between Farsi and Turkish, and provided emotional support in these often nerve-wracking offices. Moreover, as many people felt uncomfortable talking to strangers—whether social workers, healthcare providers, or lawyers—about their sexuality and gender, they asked me to "do the talking." In a support group meeting on trans refugees' access to healthcare, one trans man laughingly suggested that "everyone should go to hospital with Elif, because she does all the talking and fights with doctors until she gets the prescription for hormones."

These sustained acts of support, care, and solidarity seemed to turn me into a friend and ally, forging deeper relations of trust between us. "Doing the talking" also raised important ethical and political questions for my research. At times, I found myself actively changing the course of actions. For instance, in the morning of a sit-in organized by LGBT refugees to protest the third countries' halt of resettlement processes, in the front yard of the UNHCR's domestic partner organization, the head of security refused to let refugees in and threatened to call the police. As the only person in the crowd who spoke the language and was protected by citizenship status, I knew I had to step in. I "did the talking," first by politely asking for permission and then by "reminding him of refugees' right to protest" as well as "of the UNHCR's obligation to protect refugees" with a determined and slightly antagonistic tone, until he finally agreed to let us in. In such moments, when what was at stake was to defend refugees' rights—whether their access to hormones or their right to protest—I actively "participated" rather than passively "observing," while being cognizant of the fact that my participation was likely to change the dynamics I attempted to observe.

However, not all of "the talking" I did was in line with my political convictions. Given my fluency in English and background in gender, sexuality, and refugee studies, many people asked me to help them prepare case verification files submitted to Canadian NGOs for facilitating their resettlement. Browsing hundreds of personal photos and brainstorming with people about which images could make their identities legible to those NGOs, my eyes became trained to notice the elements that would count as "proof" of non-normative sexuality and gender. During those acts of curation, I often became complicit in the reproduction of universalizing identity categories and White, visible, middle-class gay and lesbian aesthetics. I also found it extremely challenging to turn people's personal stories into coherent, credible, and morally appealing narratives of "persecution" without reiterating the binary construction of Iran and Turkey as the backdrop of violence and oppression and the U.S. and Canada as bastions of modernity, rights, and freedoms. Indeed, countless hours I spent at my laptop to write those narratives of violence made me realize that it is very difficult, if not impossible, to survive the violence of borders unless one surrenders to the hegemonic representation of queer asylum as an escape from "repression" to "liberation" (Luibhéid 2008; Manalansan 2003; Murray 2016b; Puar 2007; Shakhsari 2014).

"Do we call them lesbians?": Compulsory heterosexuality and its discontents

Zahra left Iran in 2010 after being severely beaten up by her ex-husband, father, and brother for having a girlfriend. Five months after her arrival, she brought her ten-year-old son to Turkey through human smugglers. During her refugee status determination (RSD) interview with the UNHCR, Zahra was asked intrusive questions, such as if she "has sex with [her] girlfriend in front of [her] son." The UNHCR eventually found that it was unlikely for Zahra to be lesbian because she had been married to a man in Iran and has a son. Similarly, Kiana, mother to a thirteen-year-old daughter, mentioned that during the RSD interview she was repeatedly asked how she felt when she had sex with her ex-husband and why she left him. "I told [the interviewer] that my family forced me to marry, that it was not my choice. But he kept asking if I still like men. I didn't know how I could convince him that I am only attracted to women."

These encounters demonstrate how UNHCR's refugee status determination processes rely on the presumption of what Rachel Lewis (2010: 430) calls "straight until proven otherwise," whereby heterosexuality is assumed and enforced by asylum adjudicators. The UNHCR Guidelines (2012: 16) advise against the use of stereotypical images of sexual minorities in determining refugee status, stating that self-identification as LGBTI should be sufficient to indicate one's sexual orientation and/or gender identity.

However, asylum applicants who had been married in their home countries and/or have children are often denied asylum (Bennett 2014; Lewis 2010; Tremblay 2014) based on the failure to conform to common Euro-American perception of lesbians as "young, unmarried, childless, and independent of their families" (National Center for Lesbian Rights 2006: 4).

The experiences of Zahra and Kiana also point us to the problematic use of "immutability" as a guiding principle for the assessment of LGBTI asylum cases. During their RSD interviews, they were asked when they "found out" or "realized" that they are lesbian; when they "came out" to their families; and when they had their first romantic or sexual relationship with a woman. By interrogating the applicant's sexuality deep into her childhood and first sexual experiences, asylum adjudicators seek to map a linear and causal development of sexuality (Berg and Millbank 2009) and to establish a clear boundary between homosexuality and heterosexuality (Hinger 2010; Walker 1996). The search for innate, fixed, and visible sexual categories neatly divided between homosexual/heterosexual and outed/closeted sexuality, however, is often unable to capture the lived experiences of refugees. Many of my interlocutors mentioned that marriage to a man was a way to protect themselves, as their safety in Iran had depended upon hiding their attraction to women. Yet, they are often found ineligible for asylum because their previous heterosexual marriages are perceived as an aberration from an "immutable" and "innate" lesbian identity.

At the same time as they register with the UNHCR, refugees must lodge a parallel asylum application with the Turkish Directorate General of Migration Management (DGMM). Like the UNHCR, the DGMM also conducts its own RSD interviews, assessing the "credibility" of refugees' narratives and the "authenticity" of their sexual orientation and/or gender identity. Unlike UNHCR's interviews, however, many people found RSD interviews conducted by the DGMM to be less challenging. This is partly because, as a relatively new institution established in 2013, DGMM has not yet developed as complex and sophisticated case-assessment methods as the UNCHR's, and partly because DGMM officers do not have enough expertise and knowledge to scrutinize refugees' claims.[4] Kiana, for instance, told me that her interview at the UNHCR lasted five hours while DGMM's interview lasted less than half an hour: "They didn't even know what lesbian is. What could they possibly ask me?"[5]

I should note, however, that refugees' sexualities are a constant object of suspicion and investigation during their encounters with DGMM officers outside the official interview context. Upon their registration, the Turkish state assigns refugees to one of the small towns located mostly in the interior of the country, where there is no freedom of movement; refugees have to "sign-in" regularly at the local DGMM offices via iris and fingerprint scanners, and even a small trip to a nearby town could put them under the risk of deportation unless they secure a "travel permit" from the local DGMMs. In the summer of 2018, Kiana visited the local DGMM office to request a travel permit for a short vacation to the Mediterranean coast with her daughter. The DGMM officer who issued the travel permit asked her, out of the blue, "Are you sure you are not bisexual?" "Yes, sir, I am sure. I am lesbian," said Kiana, trying to maintain her composure in the face of this abrupt and intrusive question that had nothing to do with the travel permit. Yet, the officer seemed unconvinced. He put his hands on his head and mused for a while. Then, he called his co-worker sitting at the next desk and asked, "Do we call them lesbians if they were married before?"

This uninformed DGMM officer's question demonstrates how even those people who were granted "recognized refugee" status repeatedly find themselves in the position of being cast as "illegitimate" and "inauthentic" figures, whose sexualities are persistently questioned and disbelieved as they navigate bureaucratic and administrative processes of the asylum system in Turkey. Furthermore, refugees like Kiana are likely to be perceived as "fake cases" by many members of the LGBT refugee community. I have observed that some women choose to hide their past marriages from other refugees, and sometimes even from their close friends and partners, because they are afraid of being labeled as "fake" lesbians. Those who openly talk about their previous marriages, on the other hand, often emphasize that they had very little, or no, sexual contact with their ex-husbands, that the sexual encounters were not consensual, and that they did not enjoy it when they were forced to have sex. These confession-like statements demonstrate refugees' attempts to prove their "authenticity" in the face of a community that tends to police one another by employing certain heteronormative assumptions that echo those used by asylum adjudicators (Shakhsari 2014).

Yet, some refugees also resist this communal tendency to disbelieve their "authenticity." Kiana, for instance, nominated herself as the representative of lesbians in her city. "They might not vote for me, but I don't care. I have nothing to prove to anyone. I am a *full* lesbian and a proud mother," she stated with confidence. She has indeed become the representative of lesbian refugees, and eventually "the mother" of the larger LGBT refugee community. However, she still has to fight gossip and rumors about her "fake" case. While she mostly shrugs off these rumors, she also gets angry sometimes: "I received recognition from the UNHCR only three days after my interview. If I were not a *full lesbian*, how could I get recognition so easily?" The first time I heard this, I was perplexed by Kiana's appeal to the UNHCR as an expert witness to add credibility to her sexual orientation, since it was the very same institution that contested her "authenticity" during her interview. However, as I heard her repeatedly making this argument, I came to understand that Kiana has nothing but her words and a UNHCR-issued recognition letter to prove her lesbianness—and she resorts to the UNHCR letter to credibly outweigh the doubt caused by her previous marital status and motherhood.

As refugees' oral narratives become considered less and less credible, the asylum system relies on a growing demand for evidence of "authenticity," sought through refugees' intimate documents (White 2014), and reports written by country experts (Good 2007), medical experts (Fassin and Rechtman 2009), caseworkers (Cabot 2014), or lesbian and gay organizations (Murray 2016b; Shakhsari 2014). Together, these documents work as "ambiguous mechanisms of administrative control" (Murray 2016a: 83). That is, while they are meant to support refugees' claims by proving their "credibility" and "authenticity," they simultaneously reflect the asylum system's foundational assumption of the refugee as a "potential fraud" (Fassin and Rechtman 2009: 273). Kiana's use of her UNHCR recognition letter to prove her *full* lesbian identity to other refugees is illustrative of how the transnational asylum system's practices contribute to a broader discourse that enables and reinforces the dismissal, denial, and distrust of lesbian refugees who were married and/or who have children. In order to (re)claim their identities, people like Kiana often have no choice but to make use of the very same discourses and practices that tend to police and discredit their and others' identities.

"Homophobic violence" and "native others"

In February 2018, the executive director of an Iranian NGO based in Canada was on a mission trip to Turkey, where he met LGBT refugees living in different cities. His organization was planning to initiate a fundraising campaign for lesbian refugees in Turkey. As he explained to me, this was a much-needed and timely campaign when the world, through #timesup and #MeToo movements, was showing solidarity with women who have been subjected to discrimination and harassment. In the city where I lived, he held private, thirty-minute consultation sessions with refugees. After the consultation sessions ended, he shared some lesbian refugees' stories with me, asking for my help to turn them into a campaign text.

One of these women was Baran, a refugee in her mid-forties. At the age of twenty, Baran was arrested by police for being lesbian, and the court sentenced her to be stoned to death. Her family managed to save her from prison and the death sentence by bribing the prison guards and the judges, yet they forced her to marry a man in order to "cure" her homosexuality. She stayed in an abusive marriage for years until she fled Iran and arrived in Turkey in 2016. The executive director explained: "She has a compelling story, but she was rejected by the UNHCR. Do you know why? Because she told the interview officer that she is bisexual. Apparently other refugees told her that she *cannot* be lesbian because she was married and has a child. They advised her to introduce herself as bisexual."

As with Zahra and Kiana in the previous section, Baran's story sheds light on the LGBT refugee community's tendency to discredit the lesbianness of women who were married and/or have children. The rejection of her asylum claim by the UNHCR also draws attention to the fact that bisexual applicants have much more difficulty obtaining refugee status in comparison to gays and lesbians, as bisexuality challenges the notion of an innate and immutable sexuality and an essentialized homo-hetero binary (Rehaag 2009). Yet, what made Baran's story appealing for the organization's fundraising campaign was not the rejection of her asylum claim. Baran told the executive director that she was circumcised twice, at the ages of nine and twelve. In shocked response, he told me: "Can you believe she didn't share this information with the UNHCR? She didn't think this situation would be related to her asylum application. I told her to go see a doctor, make a medical report, and submit it to the UNHCR as soon as possible. The UNHCR would give her recognition and resettle her immediately with this information. She is a *perfect golden case*,[6] but she does not even know she *ought to* say she was circumcised."

In her study of the immigration system in France, Miriam Ticktin (2011) shows how humanitarian practices turn select experiences of suffering into prerequisites for protection, recognition, and citizenship. At a time when abuse and discrimination based on one's gender do not count as "morally legitimate suffering" worthy of the asylum system's recognition, refugees are forced to present "exceptional" forms of suffering, such as gay bashing, rape, female genital cutting, or "honor crimes," which are often associated with their countries of origin (Ticktin 2011: 138). That is to say, the *cultural otherness* of the violence that refugees have endured plays a crucial role in eliciting recognition and compassion from legal and humanitarian authorities. It is in this context that, while Baran's previous marriage makes her "bisexual" in the eyes of other LGBT refugees, and an "illegitimate" subject in the eyes of the UNHCR, the female genital cutting that she had undergone twice would make her a "perfect golden case" to be recognized and resettled to a third country on a faster track.

It could be argued that the period of waiting in Turkey pushes lesbian refugees to start speaking a new language; that is, the language of a "racialized and traumatized queerness" (White 2014: 81). Iranian queer diaspora organizations play a particularly important role in the construction and circulation of this language by advising refugees on how to craft their stories in a way that would elicit compassion and recognition from the UNHCR and third countries. During the same visit, the executive director also decided to feature Kiana in the fundraising campaign as a "victim of forced marriage" and "single lesbian mother." Similar to Baran, who realized that she ought to present herself as a "victim of female genital mutilation," as the executive director suggested, Kiana had learned how to make use of the categories like "victims of forced marriage" and "single lesbian mother," as she tried to verify her case with the UNHCR and Canadian NGOs. By uttering these categories that are *new* to them, refugees *translate* their complex life stories into a Western humanitarian language, on the one hand, and into morally appealing narratives, on the other, to increase their chances of being eligible for asylum and resettlement.

As much as refugees strategically resort to these gendered and racialized victimhood categories, their narratives also reproduce a mythic image of a benevolent "country of asylum" that is the bastion of sexual rights and freedoms, in opposition to a "country of origin" that is barbaric and oppressive (Shakhsari 2014). Indeed, in countless "case verification" narratives that refugees asked me to translate from Farsi to English, one thing was strikingly common: they wanted me to emphasize that their marriages were "arranged" and "forced," often highlighting the pervasiveness of this "barbaric tradition" in Iran's "culture" and asking their North American audience to "help" them resettle to a "safe" and "free" country. It is precisely these words in quotation marks we had to use that enable people to meet the transnational asylum system's expectations of LGBT refugees: to depict their country of origin through an extremely racist and colonialist lens in order to show how homophobic it is (Bhabha 2002; Solomon 2005) and to reaffirm the host countries' commitment to modernity, freedom, and human rights (Jenicek et al. 2009; Puar 2007; White 2013).

However, "racialized and traumatized queerness" (White 2014: 81) is not the only language refugees speak in Turkey. Indeed, the invocation of queerness, particularly female queerness, diminishes refugees' chances for financial aid provided by Turkish charity organizations, due not only to the discrimination based on sexual orientation but to prevalent stigmatization of divorce. Thus, people often conceal their sexuality as they reach out to local aid providers. For instance, when I accompanied Kiana to the Turkish Red Crescent (*Kizilay*), the largest humanitarian organization in the country, she asked me not to disclose her lesbian identity. Rather, we applied for financial aid on the grounds of Kiana's "widowhood" and "single motherhood." Kiana's skillful navigation of these categories—a "victim of forced marriage," a "widow," a "single mother," and a "full lesbian," depending on who her audience is—demonstrates that, during the period of waiting in

Turkey, lesbian refugees learn to *make* (and *remake*) themselves as authentic, deserving, and legitimate *within* established tropes during their encounters with various decision makers.

Disciplinary gender and visual (un)recognizability

Rosha and Samira entered Turkey as refugees in 2014. Only one week after their arrival, they began working in a small textile atelier to earn their living, as they brought very little savings with them and did not receive any financial support from their families back in Iran. Working hard and earning little, they soon failed to satisfy even their most basic needs, such as housing and food. They eventually reached out to three Iranian diaspora organizations that provide financial help to Iranian LGBT refugees. The executive director of one of these organizations interviewed them on Skype from Canada to determine their eligibility for the organization's services. After the interviews ended, she wanted to talk to Rosha privately, asking Samira to give them a minute. While Samira was waiting in the bedroom, the executive director told Rosha: "I would like to work with you. But I am not convinced that your girlfriend is a *real* lesbian." Thus, ironically enough, one partner was recognized as lesbian and found eligible for aid, while her girlfriend was denied recognition because she did not match the executive director's idea of what a lesbian looks like.

After this distressing experience, Samira started to worry about her approaching RSD interview with the UNHCR. She eventually decided to add a fabricated story of homophobic violence to her narrative and asked Rosha to cooperate with her during the interview. When Rosha worried that it might jeopardize both of their asylum applications, Samira insisted that lying is her only option: "It is easy for you to pass the interview. Everyone believes that you are lesbian, because you are butch. But no one believes me. I will get a rejection from the UNHCR just like I got a rejection from that organization." Thus, during the interview, they told the UNHCR officer that after Samira's family found out about their relationship, they beat Samira and imprisoned her in their home for months. By embellishing her story with an act of homophobic violence by her family, Samira did three things at once: (1) she strengthened her claim to be lesbian, as she thought that her self-identification was likely to be found unconvincing; (2) she proved that she has a "well-founded fear of persecution," nullifying the assumption that she is able to "act discreetly" because of her feminine appearance (Choi 2010; Millbank 2009); and (3) she met the asylum system's desire to hear stories of "homophobic violence" enacted by a "native Other"—in this case, an Iranian/Muslim household.

Samira's story highlights the critical roles played by Iranian queer diaspora organizations in shaping and transforming refugees' sexual identities and personal narratives. In the absence of effective legal and financial assistance from the UNHCR and the Turkish DGMM, refugees often reach out to these organizations to seek financial aid and legal advice on their asylum cases. Thus, they are interviewed by these NGOs long before they are given a date for the formal UNHCR interview. Given the lack of information and transparency about UNHCR's asylum processes, many refugees like Samira deduce what to say and how to behave during their official interviews from these informal encounters with Iranian diaspora organizations.

Samira's experience also highlights a broader tendency that continues to permeate many legal and humanitarian asylum agencies and queer NGOs: to associate lesbian identity with a stereotypical butch image and consequently to deem femme and feminine-looking lesbians "inauthentic" or "fake" (Lewis 2010; Tremblay 2014). As decision makers rely on the expressive and performative aspects of sexuality to "read" asylum seekers' "true" identities (Miller 2005; Walker 1996), refugees like Samira who have feminine features, such as long hair and makeup, are easily misread as straight and denied recognition.

I should mention that I myself actively participated in reinforcing a visible and stylized butch-femme binary as I helped many lesbian women prepare "case verification" files demanded by Canadian NGOs that offer private sponsorship programs. For instance, when Rosha asked for my help to choose a few photos that she could use in her application, I found myself quickly skipping the photos in which she had long hair and makeup. What I did was not a simple selection between different images; my act of curation erased a more feminine gender expression that Rosha enjoyed during a particular period of time, as I actively searched for more masculine and androgynous gender expressions. This was not because I valued them more, but because I believed that they would make Rosha's lesbianness more visually recognizable, and consequently her "case verification" easier and faster.

Such practices and discourses in which the "authenticity" of sexual identities are being articulated, represented, and evaluated not only determine refugees' eligibility for asylum, financial aid, and resettlement. They also actively shape and transform how women narrate, perform, and embody their sexualities and genders, as well as how they perceive and interpret others' identities. In 2015, the executive director of another Iranian queer diaspora organization, based in Europe, held a community meeting for lesbian refugees in Turkey. There, I was told, she imposed on participants her own understanding of who is *really* lesbian and what a *real* lesbian should look like. Many of my interlocutors recalled this meeting with both horror and sarcasm; in addition to reiterating familiar comments about long hair and makeup, the executive director also stated that those who use dildos are *not real* lesbians, for she considered the use of a dildo as an evidence of one's desire for "penetrative sex," which she equated with "heterosexual sex."

Mojde, a lesbian refugee who has been waiting in Turkey for four years, told me that, after this meeting many refugees cut their hair and stopped putting on makeup, embracing more masculine gender expressions. Furthermore, Mojde was concerned that this meeting had had a "toxic influence" on the lesbian community, as "girls have become the sex-police, trying to understand who is really lesbian and who is not" by using the executive director's standards for how *real* lesbians look, behave, and have sex. Soon after this meeting, Mojde and her girlfriend were accused of being "fake cases," for they wore two-piece swimsuits instead of the boy shorts that were expected of them, during a community trip organized by a local NGO. "All the lesbians kept staring at us as we swam. I even heard them saying 'are they really lesbians?' Fine, if wearing a bikini makes me a fake lesbian, I am a fake lesbian. At least I enjoyed the water."

Mojde's experience of being labeled as a "fake lesbian" by other refugees highlights the centrality of identifiable appearance and behavior norms to many lesbian communities (Moore 2006; Rothblum 1994). In the context of asylum in Turkey, however, these norms are not solely determined by community members themselves, but rather imposed on them by adjudicating states, the UNHCR, Canadian and Iranian queer NGOs, and even researchers like me. The more that these essentializing disciplinary norms are circulated by people with power, the more influence they exert in the consolidation of an "ideal" lesbian refugee image, redefining the possibilities for women to imagine, embody, and express their sexual and gender identities.

Conclusion: Self-making

Queer migration studies have shown how immigration/asylum is a site of construction and contestation of sexual identities. I suggest that liminal zones of asylum like "transit countries" provide critical insight into the complex relations between asylum, sexuality, identity, and identification. As I demonstrated through the case of Turkey, these "waiting rooms" have become transnational legal and humanitarian hubs where multiple state and parastatal authorities simultaneously assess refugees' asylum claims. Refugees' chances of making their way out of this liminal time-space of waiting depend on their ability to skillfully navigate disparate expectations of these institutions and organizations, each of which has a different understanding of what counts as an "authentic" identity and a "legitimate" asylum claim worthy of recognition.

I argued in this article that, during the period of waiting in Turkey, refugees continually tailor their narratives and performances to conform to certain "lesbian types" prioritized by asylum authorities, queer NGOs, humanitarian organizations, and other refugees. By doing so, they make themselves "authentic," "deserving," and "legitimate" subjects *within* established tropes of the global resettlement apparatus. These practices also rearticulate and transform how refugees imagine and embody their own sexualities and genders, as well as how they perceive and interpret others' identities. In that vein, waiting becomes a critical site of the construction, contestation, and transformation of sexual identifications.

Notes

1. The third countries that offer resettlement to LGBTI refugees are most commonly the United States and Canada, and occasionally Australia and some European countries.
2. See Sajnani's (2014) report for a critique of the Canadian immigration system's increasing reliance on private sponsorship programs that enable the government to offload its responsibility for refugee protection onto civil society.
3. See Lewis (2012) and Shakhsari (2014), who stress the need for further analysis of global and transnational articulations of non-normative sexualities when we study citizenship, immigration, and asylum.
4. See Sarı and Dinçer (2017) for a detailed analysis of the DGMM.
5. In September 2018, the UNHCR stopped its registration and RSD activities in Turkey. Since then, the DGMM has become the sole authority in registering and interviewing refugees. Although it is early to draw conclusions on this new system, I have heard from a lesbian refugee, who was interviewed by the DGMM in early 2019, that she was interrogated about her sexuality for six hours. She also told me that DGMM's interview could not translate some of the terms she used, such as "butch," "queer," and "coming out." This article, however, examines the experiences of refugees who filed their asylum claims with the UNHCR and the DGMM prior to September 2018.
6. "Golden case" is a term extensively used by refugees and Iranian diaspora organizations, referring to the LGBT asylum cases that are accorded expedited consideration for asylum in the U.S. and Canada due to their "vulnerability" (Sarı forthcoming; Shakhsari 2014).

Acknowledgments

I would like to thank the Iranian LGBT refugees in Turkey. I am thankful to Saida Hodžić; Lucinda Ramberg; the participants of the graduate student colloquium in Feminist, Gender, and Sexuality Studies Department at Cornell University, March 2018; the anonymous peer reviewers; and Eithne Luibhéid for valuable and thoughtful comments on different drafts of this article. Warmest thanks to Rebekah Ciribassi and Bruno Seraphin for their careful editing.

Funding

This research was made possible by the Wenner-Gren Dissertation Fieldwork Grant.

References

Bennett CM (2014) *Sexuality and the Asylum Process: Tthe Perspectives of Lesbians Seeking Asylum in the UK*. Ph.D. dissertation, University of Sussex.
Berg L and Millbank J (2009) Constructing the Personal Narratives of Lesbian, Gay and Bisexual Asylum Claimants. *Journal of Refugee Studies* 22(2): 195–223.
Bhabha J (2002) International Gatekeepers?: The Tensions between Asylum Advocacy and Human Rights. *Harvard Human Rights Journal* 15: 154–181.
Biehl K (2015) Governing through Uncertainty: Experiences of Being a Refugee in Turkey as a Country for Temporary Asylum. *Social Analysis* 59 (1): 55–75.
Cabot H (2014) *On the Doorstep of Europe: Asylum and Citizenship in Greece*. Philadelphia, PA: University of Pennsylvania Press.
Choi V (2010) Living Discreetly: A Catch 22 in Refugee Status Determinations on the Basis of Sexual Orientation. *Brooklyn Journal of International Law* 36: 241–264.
Crenshaw K (1989) Demarginalizing the Intersection of Race and Sex: A Black Feminist Critique of Antidiscrimination Doctrine, Feminist Theory and Antiracist Politics. *University of Chicago Legal Forum* 1: 139–167.
Fassin D and Rechtman R (2009) *The Empire of Trauma: An Inquiry into the Condition of Victimhood*. Princeton, NJ: Princeton University Press.
Good A (2007) *Anthropology and Expertise in the Asylum Courts*. New York, NY: Routledge.
Hinger S (2010) Finding the Fundamental: Shaping Identity in Gender and Sexual Orientation Based Asylum Claims. *Columbia Journal of Gender & Law* 19(2): 367–408.
Jenicek A, Wong A and Ou Jin Lee E (2009) Dangerous Shortcuts: Representations of Sexual Minority Refugees in the Post-9/11 Canadian Press. *Canadian Journal of Communications* 34(4): 635–658.
Lewis R (2010) The Cultural Politics of Lesbian Asylum: Angela Maccarone's *Unveiled* (2005) and the Case of the Lesbian Asylum-Seeker. *The International Feminist Journal of Politics* 12(3–4): 424–443.
Lewis R (2012) Towards a Transnational Lesbian Cinema. *Journal of Lesbian Studies* 16(3): 273–290.
Luibhéid E (2002) *Entry Denied: Controlling Sexuality at the Border*. Minneapolis, MN: University of Minnesota Press.
Luibhéid E (2008) Sexuality, Migration, and the Shifting Line between Legal and Illegal Status. *GLQ: A Journal of Lesbian and Gay Studies* 14(2–3): 289–315.

Luibhéid E (2014) Afterword: Troubling Identities and Identifications. *Sexualities* 17(8): 1035–1040.

Manalansan M (2003) *Global Divas: Filipino Gay Men in the Diaspora*. Durham, NC: Duke University Press.

Millbank J (2009) From Discretion to Disbelief: Recent Trends in Refugee Determinations on the Basis of Sexual Orientation in Australia and the United Kingdom. *International Journal of Human Rights* 13: 391–414.

Miller AM (2005) Gay Enough: Some Tensions in Seeking the Grant of Asylum and Protecting Global Sexual Diversity. In Epps B, Valens K and Gonzales BJ (eds) *Passing Lines: Sexuality and Immigration*. Cambridge, MA: Harvard University Press, pp. 137–188.

Moore MR (2006) Lipstick or Timberlands? Meanings of Gender Presentation in Black Lesbian Communities. *Signs: Journal of Women in Culture and Society* 32: 113–139.

Morgan D (2006) Not Gay Enough for the Government: Racial and Sexual Stereotypes in Sexual Orientation Asylum Cases. *Law and Sexuality Review* 15: 135–161.

Murray D (2016a) *Real Queer: Sexual Orientation and Gender Identity Refugees in the Canadian Refugee Apparatus*. London, England: Rowman & Littlefield.

Murray D (2016b) Queer Forms: Producing Documentation in Sexual Orientation Refugee Cases. *Anthropological Quarterly* 89(2): 465–484.

National Center for Lesbian Rights (2006) The Challenges to Successful Lesbian Asylum Claims. http://www.nclrights.org/legal-help-resources/resource/the-challenges-to-successful-lesbian-asylum-claims/ (accessed 5 September 2018).

Puar J (2007) *Terrorist Assemblages: Homonationalism and Queer Times*. Durham, NC: Duke University Press.

Rehaag S (2009) Bisexuals Need Not Apply: A Comparative Appraisal of Refugee Law and Policy in Canada, the United States, and Australia. *The International Journal of Human Rights* 13(2–3): 415–436.

Rothblum E (1994) Lesbians and Physical Appearance: Which Model Applies? In Greene B and Herek GM (eds) *Lesbian and Gay Psychology: Theory, Research and Clinical Applications*. London, England: Sage, pp. 84–97.

Sajnani R (2014) Envisioning LGBT Refugee Rights in Canada: The Impact of Canada's New Immigration Regime. http://foundationofhope.net/wordpress/wp-content/uploads/2015/02/Report-Immigration-Regime-Jan-20151.pdf (accessed 10 October 2018).

Sarı E (forthcoming) Unsafe Present, Uncertain Future: Queer and Trans Asylum in Turkey. In Luibhéid E and Chávez KR (eds) *Queer and Trans Migrations: Illegalization, Detention, Deportation*.

Sarı E and Dinçer CG (2017) Toward a New Asylum Regime in Turkey? *Movements: Journal for Critical Migration and Border Regime Studies* 3(2): 57–78.

Shakhsari S (2014) The Queer Time of Death: Temporality, Geopolitics, and Refugee Rights. *Sexualities* 17(8): 998–1015.

Solomon A (2005) Trans/Migrant: Christina Madrazo's All-America Story. In Luibhéid E and Cantú L (eds) *Queer Migrations: Sexuality, U.S. Citizenship, and Border Crossing*. Minneapolis, MN: Minnesota University Press, pp. 3–29.

Ticktin M (2011) *Casualties of Care: Immigration and the Politics of Humanitarianism in France*. Berkeley, CA: University of California Press.

Tremblay M (2014) *In Search of Protection: Sexual Minority Women in Canadian Refugee Determination*. LLM dissertation. Université de Montréal.

UNHCR Guidelines on International Protection (2012) https://www.refworld.org/docid/50348afc2.html (accessed 10 November 2018).

Walker K (1996) The Importance of Being Out: Sexuality and Refugee Status. *Sydney Law Review 18*: 568–597.

White MA (2013) Ambivalent Homonationalisms. *Interventions* 15(1): 37–54.

White MA (2014) Archives of Intimacy and Trauma: Queer Migration Documents as Technologies of Affect. *Radical History Review 120*: 75–93.

Index

Acosta, Katie L. 3, 27
Ahmed, Sara 5
Aizura, Aren 10
Akin, Deniz 7, 13, 62
Alexander, M. Jacqui 2–3
ambiguities 34, 40–41, 55, 57–58, 61, 63
ambivalences 55, 57, 61, 63, 66
Amigas y Amantes 3
Amit, Hilka 10
Anzaldua, Gloria 4, 34
aspirations 5, 16, 71–72, 74–81
asylum 12–13, 16, 62, 85–86, 91, 95, 97–98; claims 13, 86, 88, 94, 98
Australia 16, 71–74, 77–81
authenticity 10, 84–99

Beauchamp, Toby 6
Bohmer, Carol 13–14
borders, crossing 29
Borges, Sandibel 28
Boyd, Nan Alamilla 23
Brave Heart, Maria Yellow Horse 50
Burridge, Andrew 2

Cantu, Lionel 30, 32
Cardenas, Maritza 24
Carling, Jørgen 5
Chavez, Karma R. 41
China 70–81
chuguo 16, 72, 74–77, 80–81
chuguo mobility 72, 74, 80; of queer women 70–81
Collins, Francis 5
colonialist binaries 9–10
color theory 6
compulsory heterosexuality 90
Crenshaw, Kimberle 2, 22–23

Davis, Madeline 31
DeBruyn, Lemyra M. 50
Decena, Carlos Ulises 9, 47, 55, 57, 64
deservingness 87

diasporic intimacy 26
Dubrovsky, Rachel 6

Espín, Oliva 3
events 2, 49, 60–61

family, negotiating 27
female genders 3, 7–8
Ferguson, Roderick 3
fieldwork 15–16, 41, 56, 59, 62–63, 70, 88
Fortier, Anne-Marie 5

García Hernandez, Yessica 33
gender identifications 7, 73, 75
gender identities 33, 61, 86, 88, 90–91, 98
globalization 10–11, 74
Goldstein, Alyosha 4
Gopinath, Gayatri 3, 10, 57–58

Haritaworn, Jin 50
healing 15, 38–39, 42, 47, 49–51
heteronormative demands 71, 76, 80–81
Hill, Anita 22
homophobic violence 93, 96
homotolerance 55, 58–59, 66–67
Hong, Grace 3
hypervisibility 9–10, 57

immigration system 13, 42–43, 45, 94
Impossible Desires 3, 57
informants 71–81
intersectional disempowerment 22
invisibility 9–10, 55–57, 63–64, 66–67
Iranian queer diaspora organizations 85–87, 89, 94, 97

Kaufmann, Vincent 71
Kennedy, Elizabeth Lapovsky 31
Kuntsman, Adi 50

leisure spaces 15, 23, 31–33
lesbian communities 98

lesbian-identified migrants 2
lesbian-identified trans migrants 6
lesbian-identified women 13
lesbian identity 7, 12–13, 16, 43–44, 85, 93, 95, 97
lesbian Latinas 27
lesbian migrants 2–4, 6, 8, 23, 26
lesbian migrant women 3, 57–58
lesbianness 85–87, 93–94
lesbian refugees 92–94, 96–98; in transit 84–99
lesbian sexualities 3, 7, 13
lesbian women 32, 56, 97
Lewis, Rachel 6, 13, 90
LGBTQ migrant Latinas 38–51
LGBTQ migrants 42, 44, 50
LGBT refugee community 92, 94
LGBT refugees 86–89, 93–95
livability 15, 59–60, 66
Loyd, Jenna M. 2
Luibhéid, Eithne 39, 58, 87

MacDonald, Megan 50
Magnet, Shoshana Amielle 6
Manalansan, Martin 26
Martin, Fran 79
Menjívar, Cecilia 27
migrant lesbians 2–3, 14–15
migrant lesbian women 15, 55, 58
migrants 3–5, 7–9, 11–14, 16–17, 22, 24–25, 31–32, 34–35, 39–40, 42–47, 49, 56–59, 61–62
migration narratives 9
migration processes 6–7, 23, 40
migration scholarship 5
mobility 71–72, 74–76, 81
Moraga, Cherríe 28
motivations 59, 72, 76–77, 80
Muñoz, Jose Esteban 26, 40–41
Murray, David A. B. 13, 85
Muslim lesbian women 58

Naples, Nancy 6
narrators 22–23, 32, 34, 38–42, 45, 49–51
nationhood 4, 58
native others 93, 96
non-heterosexual migrant women 54–55, 58, 61, 63, 66–67

oral histories 15, 23, 25, 38

path of conocimiento 34
Peña, Susana 9
plaza 31–33
The Politics of Passion 3
Posocco, Silvia 50

post-reform China 16
post-socialist China 72, 74, 76, 81
power 2, 4–5, 7, 9, 13–15, 17, 34, 40–41, 50, 54–55, 58, 63, 66–67
power relations 14, 61, 65–66
public correctness 72, 76, 78, 80–81; politics of 72, 76, 78, 80–81

queer communities 15, 35, 47, 55, 57, 61, 63–65, 67
queer identity 23, 32, 46, 50
queer migrant bodies, policing 42
queer migrants 10, 24–25, 31–32, 34–35, 38–39, 45, 48–49, 57–58
queer migrant women 28, 55
queer migration 3, 11, 41, 71, 74
queer migration scholarship 85
queer necropolitics 50
queerness 24, 46–47, 73, 95
queer oral history 23–25
queer possibility 58
queer space 47
queer women 6, 31–32, 70–71, 74–78, 80–81; motivations 72, 77

Raboin, Thibault 12
race 2, 10, 12, 54, 58, 62, 64, 74
Ramirez, Horacio N. Roque 23
refugees 8, 12–13, 39, 57, 59, 62, 85–89, 91–99
refugee status determination (RSD) interviews 90–91, 96
resistance 7, 10, 15, 38–39, 41–42, 45, 47, 49–51, 57–58, 61, 63, 66
Rowe, Aimee Carrillo 6
Royster, Francesca T. 6

same-sex relationships 71, 74, 77–78, 80–81
Sandoval, Chela 26
Schuman, Amy 13–14
self-making 25–26, 98
sequins, finding 21, 23, 25–29, 32, 34–35
sexual identities 7, 9, 12, 22, 27, 33, 54–55, 58, 66–67, 97–98
sexualities 7, 9, 12–14, 16–17, 39–41, 43–47, 61–64, 70–72, 74–77, 79–80, 85, 87, 89, 91–92, 97–99
Shakhsari, Sima 13–14
silence 2, 9–11, 15, 39
single lesbian mother 95
Stella, Francesca 10, 58, 64
systemic violence 15, 26, 38

tacit subjects 9, 55, 57
Thiefing Sugar 3
third countries 85–86, 88–89, 94–95

Ticktin, Miriam 94
Tinsley, Omise'eke Natasha 3, 6
transnational migration 71, 78
transnational mobility 16, 71–77, 79–81
Turkey 13, 16, 84–90, 92–99

undocumented migrants 42, 44
undocuqueers 48–50

violence 2, 4, 11, 14–15, 25–28, 30, 34, 38, 45, 49–51, 86, 90, 94
visibility 9–10, 54–57, 62–67; paradigm 54, 61, 67

Wekker, Gloria 3
White, Melissa Autumn 12
workshops 47, 61

Zavella, Patricia 40